COMMENTS ABOUT THE BOOK

"Can it be this simple? Actually, a better question might be 'why have we made it so hard?' This approach is **profoundly simple**. Bottom-line – **it works** and it can change your life!"

Doug Krug
Author, *Enlightened Leadership*

"This book leads to **harmony**, **understanding** and **well-being**. It is a concise handbook on improving and creating harmonious communication."

Matthew Greenblatt
Editor, *Inner Directions Journal*

"This book can **immediately change** the quality of your life. It gives us **simple** and **effective tools** for better communicating in love, work and everyday life."

Colette Chabot
Author, journalist

"*Water the Flowers, Not the Weeds* is a **thoroughly insightful guide** for professional and layperson alike. Fletcher takes the best approaches and principles of communication and makes them **wonderfully useful** and **easy** for the readers **to apply** in their life."

Maurice Lamb
Founder, Quantum Institute

"This book **invites us to seek solutions**. It is entirely in keeping with **a vision of the management of tomorrow**."

Marcel Nolet
CEO, Nicolet-Yamaska Health Center

"This book encourages the adoption of a **philosophy of life** which is both **comforting** and **reassuring**...I strongly recommend this book to any public or private organization seeking to introduce **cooperative** and **peaceful relations** among its staff."

Michel Guay
Senior manager, CLSC La Source

"This playful book makes complex concepts fun to use as **powerful tools** to **make our lives work better** and **flow more easily**."

Bill Kauth
Founder, Warrior-Monk Training

"I strongly recommend that companies and individuals **take advantage** of this book and its knowledge of communication, conflict resolution and **ideal work relationships**. We easily succeeded in adapting this philosophy to our daily relationships."

>**Patrice Legault**
>**Treasurer, Hoechst Marion Roussel Pharmaceuticals**

"*Water the Flowers, Not the Weeds* addresses the two most challenging areas in human development, communication and relationship, and **creates a map** for navigating this uncertain territory. The process is **presented with clarity, compassion and humor** that allows for **easy learning** and **integration** in practical, immediate ways."

>**Catherine Seo**
>**Partner, Synergistic Solutions**

"**Wise, simple, practical** and **easily applicable** in personal and professional life."

>**John Gaddis, Ph.D.**
>**Social worker**

"This is a **philosophy of life** which is useful to all teamwork. Its **simple principles** are easily integrated...and the common language thus developed **permits lasting and effective cooperation**."

>**Liza Chamberland**
>**CEO, La Vallée**

"*Water the Flowers, Not the Weeds* is **immediately applicable** to our personal and professional lives **with results** that are **truly encouraging**. This book **emphasizes positive** aspects, **cooperation** and **the search for solutions**."

>**Gilles Morin**
>**Manager, Arthur Buies**

"*Water the Flowers, Not the Weeds* presents **Solution Focused Communication,** which has proved to be an **invaluable, creative** and **powerful approach** with our clients. I recommend this book to any organization where the individual plays an important role in realizing its vision and mission."

>**Aurèle Doucet**
>**Director, Nor'east Health Network**

"This book encourages a **better understanding of individuals' attitudes. It opens the way to finding solutions** in the face of resistance to change."

**The Management Committee
Laterriere Factory**

"*Water the Flowers, Not the Weeds* offers a simple and efficient model that **focuses on what goes well** and that emphasizes that **our principal clients are ourselves**! This positive approach can only be helpful in an organization such as ours in the process of change."

**The Executive Committee
Quebec Electrical Energy**

"*Water the Flowers, Not the Weeds* and Solution Focused Communication permitted us to see our reality from a new angle and to appreciate the pleasure of **seeing our world as being full of** stimulating **opportunities** rather than difficult problems."

**Jacynthe Côté
CEO, Beauharnois Plant**

"The contents of this book helped us to **increase team spirit** and to **improve** our **speed in building lasting relationships** with external clients."

**André Girard
Vice-president, ABB Engineering**

Water the Flowers
Not the Weeds

Water the Flowers
Not the Weeds

a Strategy that Revolutionizes
  • **Professional**
  • **Personal**
  • **Family**
Communication and Relationships

Fletcher Peacock

This book is a translation of *Arrosez les fleurs, pas les mauvaises herbes!*, published by Les Éditions de l'Homme, 1999.

Design and production: Donald Turcotte *Communications*
Front cover photography: Brigitte Maheux (Bavana)
Photograph of Mr. Peacock: Josée Lambert
Translation: Winnifred Peacock
Text revision: Marjorie Dunham-Landry

Published by:
Open Heart Publishing
1235 Bernard St. West, Suite 17
Montreal, Quebec
Canada
H2V 1V7
Telephone: (514) 495-3699
Fax: (514) 495-3699
E-mail: solution1@videotron.ca
Web site: www.FletcherPeacockCommunicationSolutions.com

ISBN 0-9688102-0-9

Printed in Canada

Contents

ADVICE TO THE READER

This book has been inspired by the many conferences and seminars that Fletcher Peacock has given worldwide on Solution Focused Communication.

It is presented in such a way that it addresses both hemispheres of the brain simultaneously.

You will find the theory of Solution Focused Communication presented clearly and directly so that the left brain (logical, rational and organized) may receive it. At the same time, through stories, metaphors and examples, its message is equally available to the right brain (intuitive, relational and creative), which can then adapt it to its own needs.

Certain sentence structures may sometimes seem to sacrifice the beauty of the written language. We apologize for this. Since the book has been edited directly from Fletcher Peacock's seminars and conferences, we have purposely retained the form of the "spoken word" in order to maintain the freshness, the dynamism and the enthusiasm which the author brings to his professional trainings. At the same time, we promise you that this book contains a very clear description of the transformational elements that are available to you through Solution Focused Communication.

Furthermore, by simply reading the chapter headings, the subtitles and the words purposely written in bold print, one can read, reread or simply review the principal elements of this book in only a few minutes – a fact which will make it even more inviting and practical for our readers.

Happy Reading!

ACKNOWLEDGMENTS

First of all, I would like to thank all the people and the schools of thought that have contributed to the development of my thinking: Bill O'Hanlon for his suggestions on the three generations in communication, Milton Erickson for his basic principles, Steve de Shazer and the Milwaukee school for the major development of the solution focused approach, Ken Keyes for the motto "Resistance causes persistence," Deepak Chopra for an understanding of psychosomatic medicine, Richard Bandler and his colleagues for neurolinguistic programming, Ed Oakley and Doug Krug for the ideas contained in *Enlightened Leadership*, Dudley Lynch and his colleagues for the story of the dolphins, McGill University for its teaching and for the scholarships which permitted me to develop many of the ideas presented in this work.

Secondly, I wish to thank all the organizations which have invited me to present seminars, training sessions and conferences in the world of business and in the areas of education, health and government. In particular, I would like to thank the following resource people: Danielle Bouliane, Bertrand Rossignol, Monique Tessier, Clement Michel, Louis Blanchette and Michel Guay, Luc Boivin and Aurèle Doucet.

Thirdly, I wish to thank the thousands of students who have participated in my trainings around the world. Their curiosity, their questioning and their suggestions have greatly contributed to the development and to the constant improvement in the presentation of this approach.

On a personal plane I would like to thank **my parents, Winnifred and Weston**, for their love and support. Their core values of loving service and contribution have profoundly influenced all aspects of this book. Also I would especially like to acknowledge my mother for her wonderful work in translating this book from the French original. I also recognize my sister, Helen, for her empowering and unwavering confidence and her love. Furthermore, I wish to thank my friends Sophie, Jocelyne, Helene and Ginette for the beautiful mirrors and the wonderful opportunities which they provided for me to develop and to put into practice the principles described in this book. Also, I would like to recognize all the beautiful friendships which have enriched my life: Roberto, Nancy...Suzanne, Andree...you know who you are. Thanks for your love and friendship. Thanks to Donald Turcotte for the excellent editing, the beautiful cover design and the wise coaching. Thanks also to all my "non-dualist" friends around North America.

Finally, I would like to warmly acknowledge **my very valued collaborator, Colette Chabot**. She has been instrumental in setting in motion events that have allowed people in many areas to share their gifts and talents. It is in large part thanks to her inspiration and to her talents as a writer, journalist and impresario that the boat has arrived in port and that the "concerto" has been completed.

My profound gratitude to all!

INTRODUCTION

This book is an overview, a concise description of the Solution Focused Communication approach. We suggest that it can enrich both your personal and professional life.

The principal key word of this approach is the word **cooperation,** and the two main questions which we will discuss in these pages are: **"How can we better cooperate with everybody in our life,** both professionally and personally?" And secondly, **"How can we find solutions which are satisfying for all persons concerned?"**

**Little by little this book will reveal to you
a philosophy of cooperation**

which spontaneously energizes what one wishes to create and which puts the accent on the full potential of the individual. It also permits the reader to play the game of life in an intrinsically "win-win" manner which we will refer to as "the style of the dolphin."

In Solution Focused Communication, our responsibility is to be strong supporters and cheerleaders (we lead the applause, we encourage)! That is to say, we are interested in looking for and acknowledging qualities that point to solutions for our clients, our partners, our co-workers, our students, our spouse and our children. We will provide you with **new tools, new distinctions** that will enable you to better communicate at any time and in any situation.

This book is inspired by the best techniques and the most recent concepts which have proven to be highly effective in many varied domains such as business, education, health and government. What distinguishes this from other methods, however (without excluding them), is the fact that Solution Focused Communication is **immediately applicable.**

One very important outcome of the application of these ideas is the satisfaction of accomplishing more work in a shorter period of time; this results, of course, in a lighter workload and, ultimately less stress. Solution Focused Communication thus provides a genuine **means of preventing** the all too familiar state of **professional burnout**.

You will discover in this book that each person has a unique way of communicating and cooperating with us. The question then becomes how to find the key which will unlock the door that is blocking communication and thus facilitate our relationships: employer-employee, colleague-colleague, teacher-student, parent-child, spouse-spouse.

Solution Focused Communication emphasizes the strengths and the resources of the person involved, the characteristics which permit him to create his own reality and to make his way through the normal ups and downs of life.

In this approach, we look in a positive way at the person or the organization that is experiencing difficulties. However, rather than being hindered by explanations and analyses of causes, we put the emphasis on the discovery of solutions. We look for and acknowledge the successes and the good already accomplished which in turn suggest possibilities and provide a foundation on which to build future successes.

If you are looking for "the difference that can make the difference" in your communications, you are invited to read this book. Prepare yourself to **WATER THE FLOWERS, NOT THE WEEDS!**

Chapter 1

I DO NOT HAVE THE TRUTH

As a seminar leader, I have had one peculiar characteristic: I've taken as many courses as I have given! I love to study, to discover, to learn. You might say that I'm an eternal student!

But when I discovered Solution Focused Communication, my whole philosophy of life changed. It was then that I began to realize:

I DO NOT HAVE THE TRUTH!

My life took a truly significant turn.

When I was young, I often thought that I had the truth. I recall my first job which was in the area of adult education. I was working for a group called Frontier College, in the northern region of Quebec, Canada. During the day, I worked with the railroad workers as a laborer, and in the evening, I taught English, French and Mathematics. That was twenty-five years ago. I soon discovered that the railroad workers were earning only one dollar an hour, a wage that I found very unjust. I was politically involved and these events made me quite radical. I became what we call a socialist. This movement is less popular now, but at that time **I possessed the socialist truth.**

When we have the truth, have you noticed **how hard we work** in our relationships – with our colleagues at work, with our spouse, with our children, with our clients? We have to convince, to impose our point of view on others and that is definitely hard work!

When I possessed the socialist truth, I struggled, I fought to convince, to impose my views. I subsequently moved to Western Canada, where I worked with a political party. And since I possessed the truth, I worked ten to twelve hours a day and, during the elections, fifteen hours a day, always having the truth.

At that time, the most interesting people in the party were a type of Marxist. If you want to talk to someone who feels that he or she has the truth, I suggest that you talk to a Marxist.

I then moved to another Canadian province, where I became interested in labor unions. And naturally **I now possessed the union truth.** My "mission" was to go into factories and to create unions.

At that time, I was still living in the same city as my parents. They are the most gentle people in the world; my mother is a social worker and my father a teacher and human relations consultant. A sense of beauty and of sharing flows in their veins. They love to help, to give and to contribute to the betterment of society. At that time, I thought that I had come on this earth to help people learn to love themselves, to accept themselves, to live in peace. But, since I possessed **the truth (socialist, Marxist, union),** I criticized and attacked these gentle and loving people as bourgeois, as capitalists and as exploiters of the working class. Because that's how one demonstrates love and peace, is it not? We insult the people we love, we attack them, we criticize them so that we can enlighten them!

Then I realized that perhaps I needed to find a little more inner peace before giving it to others. Accordingly, I sought out monasteries where very quickly **I possessed the monastic truth** with which I then harassed the world.

However, I was not completely foolish, not totally stupid, and I recognized the fact that **the truth had changed so many times** in my life that perhaps I did not have the truth at all! All that I really had was **a system of beliefs which were always in the process of evolving,** of being transformed and, ideally, of being improved.

What I am presenting to you in this book is not the truth. I am presenting **possibilities**. It is up to you to choose the things that suit you best and to let the rest go like water off a duck's back.

Some years ago when I was invited to speak to 350 managers, one of them said to me: "Fletcher, I really liked your talk but I found your introduction much too long, especially the story 'I do not have the truth.' " I burst out laughing, because if you have truly understood that story, you can close this book right now since the entire contents of the book rest essentially on the fact that:

I DO NOT HAVE THE TRUTH.

If I am in a meeting with five other people, I need to recognize that there are five truths there with me. If I am with one other person, I know that I have my truth but that **at the same time the other person also has his or her truth**. Therefore, in order to have a good **Solution Focused Communication** with that person, I need to slow down, to enter his world, to learn his language and to speak it. That is what we call **"pacing"** or adapting oneself to the reality and to the vocabulary of the other person.

I will give you an example which demonstrates how we can unconsciously impose our views and our values on others and how **pacing** can contribute to improving communication.

THE STORY OF NEW YEAR'S DAY

What do we do on New Year's Day? First, we wish each other a happy new year and then we begin to wish for the other person what we want for ourselves. I remember the first New Year when my girl friend's uncle shouted, "Happy New Year! I wish you good health and lots of money!" He had just revealed to me what we call **his "hierarchy of values"**: health and money. But that is not my hierarchy of values. If he had wanted to reach me he would have wished me love, inner peace and serenity, desires which better reflect **my hierarchy of values.**

Next New Year's Day I suggest that you slow down and ask your relatives, your friends, your colleagues and your clients a solution focused question: "Happy New Year! What can I wish for you?" Now you are **pacing** the other person; that is to say, you are entering the world of your companion, into **his own truth**. You are prompting him to give you the **key words** which represent **his hierarchy of values**.

The trainings and the seminars which have inspired this book were first prepared for health and educational professionals before being extended to areas of industry and commerce and to various government departments. I have been astonished, as you will also be, at the effects immediately observed by participants in their daily lives. For example, one man declared, "After your training, Fletcher, **the person with whom I was having the greatest difficulty** in my life **became the person who appeared to me to be the most interesting!**" Another person made this observation: "Mr. Peacock, since I took your course, **all my clients have changed!**" In reality, it was he himself who had changed; he was perceiving the other people in his life differently. We have an expression: **"The world is your mirror,"** a saying which the above examples illustrate well. Another participant said to me, "Before taking your course, I was already oriented toward solutions, but since I took your training, I am much **more oriented toward other people's solutions!**" These are very interesting results!

Let me share with you one of our favorite mottos in the world of Solution Focused Communication:

More and more, we do less and less!

You will discover throughout this book an emphasis on this precept: very frequently **in doing less, a great deal less, we can accomplish more, much, much more**. Indeed, it becomes terribly exhausting when we wish to impose our truth on another or on others. In **Solution Focused Communication** (a systemic approach), we see that little changes in ourselves, in our thinking, in our attitude or in our behavior can bring about important transformations in our relationships. This is true in whatever context we are functioning, whether it be at work, in social situations or at home with family members.

For this reason, among others, **Solution Focused Communication** has proven itself to be **a very efficient tool in the prevention of professional burnout.**

The tools contained in this book will also remind you that:

**You already know a great deal more
than you think you know!**

As we are **all communicators**, this is the word that I will use rather than the different terms or titles that vary according to your specific field of work or action. Thus it will be much easier for you to recognize yourself and to adapt this "communication" to your colleagues at work, to your partners in business, to your students, to your employees or to your spouse or your child.

Also, like my courses, this book is addressed to both men and women. In order not to burden the text, I will therefore utilize the word "**communicator**" as described above, and for the "other" with whom you are interacting, I will primarily use the expression "**the other person.**" This simplification of terms will serve as a way of making the application of the principles of solution focused communication as general as possible.

I must warn you immediately that I will be telling a great many stories. I would like you to consider the stories presented here as **metaphors.** For example, if I am talking about parent-child relationships, what I am saying can just as well be applied to employer-employee relations. Similarly, when I am discussing couple relationships, my suggestions may be adapted to the inter- actions between two office colleagues or two students at school, or, indeed, to two people in any situation. Understand also that this work has hypnotic qualities and that the same ideas will appear and reappear from various perspectives and different points of view.

But remember: I am presenting you with ideas or hypotheses that you can reject at any time since...

I DO NOT HAVE THE TRUTH.

Your own intuition will always be your best guide. Don't hesitate to let go of, or put aside, whatever does not work for you.

In the days, weeks, months and years to come, if there is ever a contradiction between what I have apparently suggested that you say or do and what your intuition suggests, **always follow your intuition.**

Now we are ready to enter into the heart of the subject. Let us begin with a description of the **three generations of communication**.

Chapter 2

THE THREE GENERATIONS
OF COMMUNICATION

THE FIRST GENERATION

I n the area of communication, we can distinguish three gene-rations. In the first generation, there is the profound belief that it is absolutely necessary to first find the origin of the prob-lem in order to escape from it and go on to create a better present and a better future.

This first generation is directly inspired by the Austrian psychiatrist Sigmund Freud, considered to be the father of psychoanalysis. The psychoanalytic approach assumes that we are influenced by unresolved conflicts dating from childhood and that it is necessary to understand these conflicts of the past in order to resolve the problems of today.

This is a **long-term** approach and requires months, even years of work. It also often has **a pathological basis** in which, from time to time, the communicator places labels with a negative connotation on the persons involved.

The first generation approach is based on **expertise.** The communicator (the consultant, the trainer, etc.) always knows a little more about the problem than you do, whether it concerns your business, your employee or yourself. Generally speaking, there is an impression that the consultant knows more than the client about what is good for him or her.

THE SECOND GENERATION

In North America during the fifties and sixties, the second generation of communication was invented and developed. This was a systemic approach and may be summed up as follows: regardless of the explanation of problems relating to the past, **problems** are **maintained in the present by** the **vicious circles** of the persons involved, resulting in what we might also term "dysfunctional interactions."

Let us now look at a few examples of second generation communication.

THE STORY OF THE COUPLE

A couple is meeting with a counselor. Both the man and the woman admit that they are dealing with a very big problem. The husband wishes to have more peace and quiet, so he retreats behind his newspapers. The wife, on the other hand, wishes to spend more quality time with her spouse and have more personal and emotional exchanges. Therefore, she attempts again and again to gain her husband's attention. The more she does this, the more he withdraws. The more he withdraws, the more she tries to engage him in conversation. They are beginning to consider divorce when they arrive at the counselor's office.

At this point, the responsibility of the second generation communicator is **to intervene and interrupt these vicious**

circles. That is to say, he or she must help the client, whether it be the husband or the wife, to think and/or to act in a way that is significantly different and thus break the vicious circle, the dysfunctional interaction. The emphasis then is on what is happening today, in the present moment.

A vicious circle, or dysfunctional interaction, will usually result in our **doing more of what doesn't work**.

THE STORY OF THE AMERICAN TOURIST

An English-speaking American tourist is in a restaurant in Paris, where the waiter speaks only French. The American gives his order in English. The French waiter does not understand. What does the American do? He speaks more loudly in English. But the waiter understands even less.!

THE STORY OF THE FAMILY

Another story comes from family life. It concerns parent-child relationships. We often hear a parent say "I am completely exhausted; I am at the end of my rope with this child. I can do nothing more. I do not know what else I can do with him." When the consultant asks:

"What do you do when something doesn't work with your child?"

The parent quite often replies: "I scream at him!"

"And does that work?" asks the consultant.

"No! Not at all!"

"And what do you do when that doesn't work?"

Often, very often, we hear this reply: **"I shout again – even louder."**

These are metaphors! But all this applies to us: **We get ourselves into vicious circles** with our children, with our spouse, with our colleagues at work. And often when something doesn't work **we do more of what doesn't work.** We shout harder! Isn't that so?

When I experimented with the second generation approach, I obtained more satisfying results for both the client and myself. In fact, instead of floundering about in the old problems for months or years, we were able to arrive more quickly at solutions.

I liked this **non-pathological** approach which gives results **in a shorter time**. The term "non-pathological" means that the consultant does not place negative labels on his clients. They are simply considered as human beings with human problems. This approach, as compared with that of the first generation, is less likely to present the consultant as an expert who knows all the answers to all the clients' problems.

Finally, fifteen years ago, I discovered the third generation of communication, the solution focused approach.

THE THIRD GENERATION

The third generation may be summarized simply: No matter what the explanation of a problem of the past may be, no matter how the vicious circles maintain the problem in the present, Solution Focused Communication permits us **to go directly into the future.**

We can go directly into the world of solutions, into the world of resources, without necessarily slowing down to explore and explain the problem. We can go directly into the future where the problem does not exist! But what does that mean, to go directly into the future? To explain, let me give you an example taken from the work of Milton Erickson.

THE EINSTEIN OF COMMUNICATION

Milton Erickson was a doctor, psychologist and therapist, and he was also well skilled in hypnosis. He was known as "The Einstein of communication for the twentieth century"! It was he who inspired the second generation in communication and, most importantly, the third, the generation called **"solution focused communication."**

THE STORY OF THE DEPRESSED MAN

One day Erickson was with a very difficult client. This was a man completely depressed, whom we would call a "Complainant" in the third generation. He was completely worn out by his suffering.

Erickson tried everything with this individual and nothing worked. As he had nothing to lose, he decided to use formal hypnosis. While in a hypnotic trance, the man was directed by Erickson into the future, to a time when his problem had been solved. Then Erickson asked him – still under the effect of the trance: **"What did you do** to solve your problem? **What are the solutions that you found?"**

Still in the future, still hypnotized, the client replied: "I did this! I did that! I did this and that!..." Very gently, very respectfully, very peacefully, Erickson led the client back into the present, bringing him out of his hypnotic trance. Then, repeating exactly the same words that his client had used when in a hypnotic state, he said to him: "To settle your problem, do this, do that, do this and that!"

This is how the third generation was born, the one called **Solution Focused Communication.**

29

WHY WORK?

Here is another solution focused motto: "Why work?"

Our clients, our colleagues, our employees or our students will in most cases **find their own solutions** if we, the communicators, simply ask good questions, **solution focused questions**.

SUMMARY

The three generations of communication

- **First generation:** understand the problem; explain the problem of the past. Approach: long-term, pathological, dependent on the expert (requiring time and money).

- **Second generation:** systemic approach which consists of interrupting the vicious circles in the present. Approach: more short-term than the first, non-pathological and less centered on the expert.

- **Third generation**: We send the client into the future where there are no problems, only solutions. Approach: even more short-term, non-pathological, not based on the expert, and respectful of the resources of the other. A "cheerleader" approach, where we learn to ask good solution focused questions.

We have just discovered the three generations of communication. We are going to begin now to elaborate certain principles and basic techniques of the third generation, **Solution Focused Communication (SFC).**

Chapter 3

THE SOLUTION FOCUSED
APPROACH

The solution focused approach is the best of the short-term approaches. It is neither pathological nor dependent on the expert. In effect, it is an approach of "support." And I suggest that:

WE ARE ALL CHEERLEADERS!

Let us imagine that you are a fan attending a game in a sports center. We are in the "past" as we have not yet discovered Solution Focused Communication. I, as a communicator, used to have a tendency to leap onto the ice, take the hockey player (my client) on my back and skate, often in a direction which was the opposite of the direction in which he wanted to go. This is a metaphor, but it illustrates clearly an exhausting, draining approach that is far from providing the anticipated results.

Today, I am much more a "cheerleader". I remain in the stands (it is less tiring!) and I ask the other person good, solution focused questions.

THE BEST LEADER

In the past, the best leader was the one who had the best answers. In the future, the best leader will be the person who knows how to ask the best questions!

We are all **leaders.** We are leaders in our business, in the office, in our couple, in our families, in our community and in our society.

Several years ago when I was in Russia with an international group of organizational consultants, one of my colleagues said to me, "There are two Americans who are doing work which is similar to yours!" Their names are Ed Oakley and Doug Krug. Shortly after my return to Canada, I read their book *Enlightened Leadership.* I was so impressed by one of their statements that I wish to share it with you: "In the past, the best leader was the one who had the best answers. But, **in the future the best leader will be the person who knows how to ask the best questions**." That expresses very well the idea of the fan in the hockey stands, the famous cheerleader.

We often hear of business people who state that their work consists essentially in "motivating the key resource people" of their businesses. But how many of them know how to ask really good questions?

In the solution focused approach, we affirm that:

The quality of your life (personal, professional) is proportional to the quality of the questions that you ask.

Further, **the quality of your organization is directly proportional to the quality of** the questions that the members of the team (managers, employees) ask.

Naturally, the questions that you ask are inspired by your basic **beliefs** and by your fundamental **presuppositions.**

Therefore, according to this approach, it is very important to be aware of the presuppositions that we hold. It is essential that we understand that **our beliefs create our attitudes** which, in turn, profoundly influence our experience of "reality" and consequently the type of questions that we are going to ask.

In the preceding chapter, we described the three generations of communication. It is important, at this point, to emphasize that **in the first, the second and the third generations, the beliefs (and the attitudes) are totally different! Therefore, understandably, the questions that we are going to ask will also be totally different!**

For **the first generation** of communicators, the basic belief, the presupposition, is that it is absolutely necessary to understand the problem. Therefore, the communicator asks many questions about the problem. The result, from time to time, is what I call **negative hypnosis**. By that I mean that **in talking a great deal about the problems, we reinforce** and we worsen the situation. Furthermore, this often creates what I call **"negative blame."** The result is often invalidating, guilt-inducing, and "de-energizing" for the other person.

For **the second generation**, the belief is that it is absolutely necessary to understand the vicious circles in order to resolve them. A great deal of time is needed to grasp and break these circles. This also can become **negative hypnosis** and/or **negative blame**. It can really drain the energy of your employees, your colleagues, your spouse or your children.

33

For **the third generation,** we emphasize human potential and solutions and thus avoid these pitfalls. We ask: **What** do you want to create? **How** can you move toward this goal?

THE STORY OF UNEMPLOYMENT

When I was facilitating a three-day seminar for about sixty teachers, the principal of the school said to me:

"Fletcher, I am the mayor of my town. We have a big unemployment problem. The government gave us a $60,000 grant to study the problem. Two years later, we have a book that is two inches thick which enables us to understand the problem thoroughly. We have no solution, but, my God, do we understand the problem!" This is first generation.

Recently, a director of social services called me. "I have big problems in my organization," he said. "A great many conflicts. I even have a of problem of morale on my hands. I am willing to pay you for six months to study the problem." I burst out laughing. Of course, I lost the contract. I did not do enough pacing with him. I was unconsciously imposing my third generation "truth" on someone who was still in the first.

A PROBLEM OF PRODUCTION

In *Enlightened Leadership,* my colleagues Ed Oakley and Doug Krug relate the story of an American company which had signed a five-year contract to deliver software to a large multinational. If the employees completed the project earlier than forecast, the company would receive a bonus amounting to millions of dollars. But if they took longer, the firm would have to pay a penalty of several million dollars.

Unfortunately, after two years of work, the company was fourteen months behind schedule. Imagine the stress of the managers in that organization!

The executives of the company and the managers came regularly to the factory to attempt to find the problem and to correct it. **Why** is your production plan not working as planned? **Why** are you behind schedule? All the questions asked at every level of the business began with the word **why**. This is understandable:

First generation = Explanation of the problem

The situation was still the same when my two American colleagues arrived to consult to the business with **their third generation, Solution Focused Communication strategies.** They taught all the members of each team to first ask **the two following solution focused questions:**

1. What is the goal?
2. How can you move minimally toward the goal?

The first question: **"What is the goal"** once clarified, my two colleagues then asked question number two: **"What small thing can each member of the team do now to advance a little bit toward the goal?"**

This exercise had the effect of totally reversing the direction of the inquiry, and the employees succeeded in delivering the product in only four years, a result which permitted the company to collect a bonus of several million dollars!

Permit me to repeat: **The quality of your life** (personal, professional, organizational) will be **proportional to the quality of the questions that you ask**. That is why, throughout this book, we are presenting you with many questions of the third generation, **questions of quality, solution focused questions.**

We have seen how Milton Erickson obtained excellent results working with a depressed patient who had been wallowing in his suffering for many years. He hypnotized him and sent him into the future where the problem no longer existed.

We do not have to use formal hypnosis or Ericksonian hypnosis to obtain good results. Because:

We are all hypnotists.

Every question that we ask ourselves or others **orients** your attention or that of others. If I ask: "Why do you have a problem?" I am orienting your attention toward the problem. In **the solution focused approach,** we go toward the future. The communicator directs the other person toward solutions.

As a management consultant, I give about forty training seminars a year. Generally, I am very pleased. However, each year, there are one or two sessions where the participants are less enthusiastic.

SOME QUESTIONS FOR DIFFICULT SITUATIONS

In the past, I used to ask myself first generation questions: "**Why** does the room seem less enthusiastic? **Why** has a certain participant asked a question which implied dissatisfaction? **Why** have I been unskillful?"

Now I am more inspired by the third generation, Solution Focused Communication.

Therefore, I prefer to ask the two following questions:

1. "**What am I learning** in this organization which seems to me to be more difficult?" Or again: What am I learning from this client who seems to me to be less satisfied?

2. "**What can I do differently in the future in order to obtain better results,** more satisfying for all persons concerned?"

This approach does not cause feelings of guilt or blame for me and for others. It is an approach of abundance. Do you see, hear or feel the difference in these third generation, solution focused questions?

THE MIRACLE-QUESTION

Erickson used formal hypnosis to take his client into the future. We do not need to do this because we are using **simple solution focused questions** in order to obtain the same results. The first question of this approach is the **miracle-question**.

There are many ways of asking the miracle-question. You will find the most appropriate form for yourself, your colleagues, your collaborators or the members of your family. You can say, for example: "**If everything were going well for you in your business, in your office or in your family,** (or, if things were going 'a little bit less badly'), **what would be different?** How will you **know** that it is different? What will you **see**? What will you **hear**? What will you **be doing**? What will you **feel**? What are you going to notice if the problem is no longer there, if the solution has been found?"

In your personal life, with your spouse, with your child or with other members of your family, you can ask questions in a more imaginative way. After a little talk with the person in difficulty, you might say to him: "I have a question which may seem a little farfetched, a little bizarre; it is called the **miracle-question**. Suppose that tonight, during your sleep, the magic fairy comes with her magic wand. She waves it and all your problems disappear. When you get up tomorrow, and in the days and weeks to come, **how are you going to know that a miracle has taken place?** What are you going to see? to hear? to feel? to do? What is going to demonstrate to you that the problem has been replaced by a solution?"

37

AND WHAT ELSE?

The question: "And what else?" allows the person to make **as rich a description as possible** of the desired solution. The act of describing in detail a future in which the problem is already resolved helps him to create the **expectation** that the problem will be solved. **This expectation,** once created, can help the client to think and to act in a manner which will **lead toward the accomplishment** of the expectation. We are in the process of **watering the flowers.**

No matter how you choose to formulate the miracle-question, **the goal** and the result of this question are to **project the person** in difficulty **into the future** where he or she begins **to see, to hear and to feel** what he wishes to happen instead of resisting what he does not want.

Instead of attacking the problem, we **"energize" the solutions**. These are not at all the same thing. Energetically they are very different.

To ask the miracle-question, choose the form with which you are most comfortable. You can adapt it to your needs of the moment as well as to your personality and to that of the other person. In one big factory, I noticed that a senior manager posed the miracle-question in this way:

"If you obtain the ideal result, what will you notice?"

I also suggested to certain managers forms like:

"If everything were going better in the business, in the organization and for the whole team, **what will it be like? What will have happened? What is going to happen?"**

I taught a teacher how to formulate the miracle-question for his students who were considered difficult:

"If everything is going better for you at school in mathematics, what will be different? How will you have improved your mastery of this material? How will you feel about school?"

WATER THE FLOWERS...NOT THE WEEDS!

 If there are flowers on the cover of this book, it is to remind you that **we are all gardeners.** We have chosen to water the flowers, the seeds...not the weeds!

PLACE YOUR ATTENTION ON WHAT YOU WANT TO SEE EXPAND!

After a seminar that I gave to 250 managers, half of them bought a watering can. They put them, different sizes and different styles, in plain sight in their offices in order to remind themselves that they were gardeners and that their job was to water what was working well in their organizations and in their personal life. "Energize" what is positive and what works!

It was at that moment, I think, that I decided to entitle my book:

WATER THE FLOWERS...NOT THE WEEDS!

At about the same time another subtitle came to mind: **Suffering is Optional.**

This does not mean to deny suffering. I know that there is suffering everywhere on the planet. At this time, there are more wars on the earth than there have ever been in the entire history of the human race. Three quarters of the planet is hungry. I do not deny this, but I have observed that in our daily lives we human beings have a tendency to resist a great many things. When I say that suffering is optional, I mean that if we learned to resist less the events and people in our life, this could perhaps contribute to the diminishing or even to the disappearance of much of the suffering. (See chapter 10.)

The idea of watering the flowers, the grains, the seeds, is positive hypnosis. We are going to energize what we wish to create for ourselves, for our office colleagues, for our clients, for our spouse, for our children.

MEMORIES IN THE FUTURE!

We all have what is called a "time line," that is a sequence of places where we file our memories in space. To experiment, try to visualize a rather joyful, or neutral, memory of yourself when you were six years old.

Imagine that there is an invisible screen in front of you. The place where your eyes go when you have found your memory will be the place where you will file this memory in space.

Do not take my word for it. To verify this theory, move your eyes on the imaginary screen and try to visualize your memory elsewhere; you will notice that the image of the memory is clear in only one spot.

We have memories, plans and projects as much in the future as in the past. These memories in the future are like **expectations – self-fulfilling prophecies.**

In the world of education, a student might say: "I have never liked school and I never will like it!"

Or perhaps: "I have never been good in math and I never will be." These are **memories** of the past projected **into the future**.

My uncle's father died at the age of eighty years. My uncle, who is seventy eight years old, has told us many times: "I also am going to die at eighty years of age." He is beginning to have repeated heart attacks. He is preparing to die at the age of eighty. A memory in the future!

The bad news is that we all have **negative, pessimistic, dysfunctional beliefs and memories** that we have projected into the future.

The good news is that **nothing is cast in stone**. The good news is that with the miracle-question, we can all travel on the time line. **Our miracle-question** can help us to transport ourselves into the future where we can then replace **our beliefs**, our presuppositions, our negative, pessimistic, dysfunctional memories with **memories that are optimistic, positive and functional**. If things were going well in business or at school, what would be happening? If things were going well with your partner, in your marriage, with a difficult client, with a difficult child, what would it look like? And suddenly you are **watering the flowers**. You are "energizing" the things that you want to have happen.

An example that I like very much is that of the Canadian diving champion, Sylvie Bernier, who won the gold medal at the Olympic Games in Los Angeles in 1984. "Before participating in the Games, I had already won that gold medal a thousand times," she said. She had stored up **memories of the future**. This is **creative visualization**. "I saw myself in the act of diving, of coming out of the water, of having good results. I saw myself going up on the podium, receiving the medal..." We also have this possibility for ourselves, for our clients, for our friends, for members of our family, of projecting ourselves into the future. The miracle-question propels us there.

CONCLUSION

In this chapter, we have discussed the importance of our presuppositions and of our basic beliefs. We have shown that the basic beliefs of the three generations of communication are significantly different. We have also seen how these distinctions in beliefs generate important differences in our style of intervention.

In the next chapter, we will continue to explore the principal presuppositions of the third generation: **the metabeliefs.**

Chapter 4

THE METABELIEFS

We are all communicators in different areas of our lives. That is why, to begin with, we are going to identify the principal person we can help...at all times!

WHO IS THE PRINCIPAL PERSON WE ARE ABLE TO HELP

It is yourself...at all times! In fact, if you are faced with a family conflict, or perhaps a severe professional crisis, and you are not in a "resource state," (that is to say, not in full possession of all your abilities), you need to slow down **to take care of yourself**. If you are angry or depressed, discouraged or afraid, if you are not at peace with yourself, you do not have access to all your resources, to all the possibilities.

ENLIGHTENED EGOISM

What do we mean by "enlightened egoism"? This means that we need to **take care of ourselves first in order to take better care of others**. We need to **bring ourselves back** to what we call **"a resource state"** before intervening. In Solution Focused Communication, we consider this phase very important: **Slow down to speed up!**

Here is a prayer which may be called upon in dark times, the origin of which is attributed to different human movements, most recently to Alcoholics Anonymous. Reciting it can gently recall for you the importance of reconnecting with the inner peace which is your best resource.

THE SERENITY PRAYER

**Lord, give me the courage to change
the things that I can change,
the serenity to accept the things that I cannot
change
(for the moment...)
and the wisdom to recognize the difference.**

Recently, by chance, I met the director general of an organization who had taken a seminar on **Solution Focused Communication** (SFC). I asked him what, from his recollection of his experience, affected him the most. What was the aspect of **SFC** which he had found the most useful in his life in general and, more particularly, in his life as a manager. He replied: "Without doubt, **the Serenity Prayer**. I no longer push, I no longer struggle against the things that I cannot change – for the moment." It is truly a prayer for the prevention of professional burnout.

THE HORSE STORY

 From one point of view, this book (and the trainings which inspired it) can be thought of as **a series of stories – a series of metaphors** – which illustrate the important points of SFC. Among all these stories, there are three major ones.

The first which was recounted in the first chapter is called **"I do not have the truth!"** The second story comes from Milton Erickson. It is **the horse story**.

When Milton Erickson was fifteen years of age, he was playing with a friend on his father's farm in Wisconsin. One day, a stray horse ran onto the family property. Erickson immediately jumped on the horse. His companion shouted: "What are you doing on that horse? You don't know him! He can be very dangerous!" "Yes, that's true, but I am curious!" Erickson replied.

He gently guided the horse toward the little road in front of the farm. The horse began to trot, then wandered toward the ditch to graze on the grass. Very gently, very respectfully, very peacefully, Milton Erickson brought the horse back onto the road where he galloped several minutes before entering the ditch again on the other side of the road.

One more time, Erickson very gently and respectfully led the horse back onto the road. Then they walked along about fifteen minutes before the horse once again strayed into the neighboring field.

Erickson once more brought the horse onto the road. This continued for several hours until they arrived at a fork in the road whereupon the horse began to gallop at great speed. Very quickly, he arrived at a farm where he stopped sharply in front of an old farmer who was working with his machines.

The farmer raised his head and said: "This is amazing, this is marvelous! This is my horse! This is my horse! How did you know that this was my horse?" And Erickson replied: **"It is not I who knew. It is the horse!"**

And that is how we do good **Solution Focused Communication**! Often it is not I who knows, it is the person whom I wish to help (my client). It is not I who knows, it is my associates or my partner, it is my spouse or my child. What was I doing in the past? I was jumping onto the field, I was taking the horse on my back and I was walking, very often in a direction in which he did not wish to go. Have you ever done that? Have you ever carried the horse?

MORE AND MORE WE DO LESS AND LESS! WHY WORK?

This is another of my favorite **SFC** mottos. Do you know how much a horse weighs? Twelve hundred to two thousand pounds! That is a lot of pounds on your back. And a great many people carry not only the horse, **they carry the whole stable**: the stable of families, of friends, the stable of office teammates, the stable of employees, etc. Do you recognize yourselves?

I often meet groups, organizations which have adopted the **Solution Focused Communication approach**. Each time, inevitably, I receive the same comments. First, they say that **they are agreeably surprised by the strengths, the resources and the solutions** of the people around them which, until now, were unsuspected. Secondly, they tell me: **"I carry the horse a great deal less!"**

The metaphor of the horse is very rich. Often the person who is confiding his difficulties strays into the field of problems. That is the **unique way of cooperating** with us that he has found. Our responsibility as a solution focused communicator (third generation, cheerleader) is to **lead the horse back onto the road of solutions**, the road of strengths, of resources, of good goals.

THERE IS NOT JUST ONE SOLUTION, THERE ARE THOUSANDS!

When we no longer carry the horse, we are cheerleaders. We remain in the stands and **ask** third generation quality **questions**, solution focused questions. These questions permit our colleagues, spouse or any other person **to find the solution that is most appropriate for everyone**. We encourage, we nurture, we strengthen the solution and we collaborate in its happy realization. If it is the other person, for example, who finds the solution, then that person will certainly be much more highly motivated and inspired to implement this solution because it is his.

When I was younger, I was trained to be an expert. I was an expert of the first and of the second generation. It was my job to help the client as quickly as possible. I used to offer an expert solution and when the client agreed to my expert solution, I was very happy. The client also! Everyone was happy!

When the client did not accept my expert solution of the first or the second generation, it often happened that I was frustrated and even a little discouraged. The client as well! And, from time to time, **I negatively labeled this person**: "You are **resistant**! You are not cooperating. You are **difficult**! You are absolutely **not motivated**." Those are the principal unflattering labels that I used to use to describe a client who was not a "Customer" of my solution, my truth.

THE EVOLUTION OF SOLUTIONS

Today more and more, I do less and less. I become acquainted with the situation of the other person, I know the state of his problem and I know his goal.

Further, I know – you probably know this also – that often a problem which is in the process of being resolved does not evolve toward a solution in a straight line. That is indeed very rare. It goes

47

wns. It rises and falls, and sometimes it de-
ay before it rises again. Sometimes an illness
worse before the patient's health improves.

)F THE EVOLUTION OF SOLUTIONS

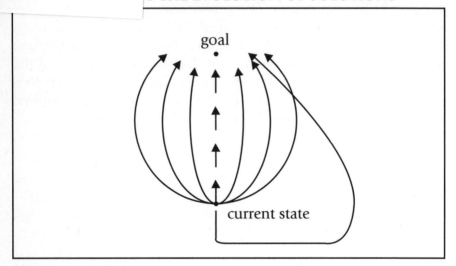

There is not only one solution, there are thousands!

If you look at the diagram above of the development of solutions, you can see that there are many ways of going from the state
of the problem, the client's current state, toward the goal, toward
the solution state. In fact, **there is not only one solution, there
are thousands**.

The story of Erickson's horse teaches us that it is not we who
choose the horse's path, nor his speed. We do not decide. Cooperating, pacing, **accepting the route of the other person often speeds
up the journey**. Remember: This approach (SFC) is based on the
principle that **"I do not have the truth!"** Such an attitude permits
us to be a great deal more open to the truth of the other person
and to the solutions that he may be able to find.

If I blame him, I am making him guilty, I am devaluing him
for not accepting my solution. I deprive him of his resources and

I enter into conflict with him. In the approach of the third generation, we know very well that regardless of what the other person does, **he has his unique way of cooperating with us**.

THERE ARE NO PROBLEMS...ONLY OPPORTUNITIES!

Do you know any people who never have personal or professional problems? When we study Chinese, we discover that a problem is an opportunity. The **Chinese** language is based on **ideograms**, word images. It is interesting to discover that the ideogram for the word **"crisis"** (or **"problem"**) is exactly the same as that for the word **"opportunity."**

EXERCISE

- We are going to do a little exercise here. I would like you to sit comfortably, close your eyes and repeat the following sentence ten times. "I have a big problem!" Observe closely what you are experiencing physically and emotionally. Notice carefully the effect that this sentence has on your body and on your emotions. Let's go!

- Generally, on the physical plane, this exercise has the following effects: The back curves, the shoulders fall, a frown appears, the heart beats a little more quickly, the smile disappears, the jaw contracts and the breathing can become difficult. On the emotional plane, people often become nervous, sad or distressed when doing this exercise.

- Stretch a little, get up and get yourself a glass of water if you want to, then we are going to do the exercise again. Settle yourselves comfortably again, close your eyes, then

49

repeat the following sentence ten times: "I have a beauti-ful opportunity! I have a beautiful opportunity..." Once again, observe the effects that this sentence has on your physical and emotional state!

CHINESE IDEOGRAM

There are no problems (crises), only opportunities.

When I have done this exercise in a large auditorium, I see lovely smiles appearing. Bodies become slack, shoulders and jaws relax. A state of inner well-being is established. This phrase **vital-izes** people, injects them with energy.

If you are the visual type and I say to you: "You have a big problem," you will see darkness or blackness. If I say: "You have a wonderful opportunity," that is a little more **brightening** to your inner vision, isn't it?

We have just done what we might call an **exercise in autohypnosis**. I suggest, and this is confirmed scientifically, that **each word is an anchoring**, that is to say, it has the power to create a state. To repeat it is to create a trance state, a hypnotic induction. What does that mean? According to Deepak Chopra, doctor and founding director of the Body-Mind Center in California, **each word and each syllable of every word can set in motion biochemical** and **physiological reactions in our body**. These reactions affect our physical and emotional state. Positive words affect us positively, and negative words affect us negatively.

Ideally, the exercise permits you to experiment directly with these effects. Consequently, we can state that **it is important to choose our words well** both for those around us and for ourselves. It is equally important to choose our images carefully.

THERE ARE NO FAILURES, ONLY LEARNINGS!

From this perspective, it is necessary to make some changes in our vocabulary, notably our use of the word "failure." Do you know that for fifteen years, I have not experienced a failure in my life? No, only learnings. Such a perspective changes our relationships in life and in the world, I assure you! In SFC, we say that there are **no failures, only learnings**.

Speaking of "big failures" has powerful effects on the body and on the emotions. You can repeat the exercise that we have just done with the words "problem" and "opportunity" using the words "failure" and "learning." While repeating the sentence "I am having a big failure!" you will feel again at some point that it is de-energizing, devaluing and even depressing. On the other hand, when we use the sentence "I am having a great learning," the experience becomes neutral or even positive and energizing.

PLACING ONESELF IN A RESOURCE STATE!

Recently, a director general who had previously taken my course told me this story: "Fletcher, I was leaving a meeting of my board of directors. I was discouraged. I said to myself, "My God, I have failed." But suddenly, this SFC thought came to me: 'No, no, this

51

is **not a failure**, it is **a learning**." This man immediately felt better. He continued practicing Solution Focused Communication with **his principal client**, himself.

He asked himself **the two SFC questions for difficult situations**:

1. What have I learned?

2. How am I going to act differently in the future?

And that took him out of his depression. Reacting in this way does not mean a denial of reality. This man was discouraged, but in asking himself what he had learned, he placed himself in an open state, a resource state. "How am I going to behave differently at the next meeting of my board of directors in order to obtain results that are more satisfactory for everyone?" He asked himself the miracle-question. **He projected himself into the future**, to a future that was better for everyone. Here is another use of the metabelief: There are no failures, only learnings!

THIS MOMENT IS PERFECT

The situation in which you find yourself at this moment is absolutely perfect for your growth and development.

Another metabelief of SFC is inspired by Milton Erickson. He compared human beings to **plants and flowers in the process of blossoming**. A plant or a flower can be damaged or hurt, can experience difficulties and yet can still blossom. And, says Erickson, **"the situation in which you find yourself at this moment is** absolutely **perfect for your learning**, for your opening, for **your blossoming."**

We are constantly moving toward a transformation, toward healing. You are going to learn and you are in the act of learning something that you will be able to use in the future to make your life better. The flower is in the act of evolving, of blooming in its own unique way.

Erickson continues: "If we place the **emphasis on what is positive**, on the little movements that take place in a good direction, we are going to amplify these improvements and this in turn will **create more cooperation** with the other person."

THE QUALITY OF YOUR LIFE IS DIRECTLY PROPORTIONAL TO THE QUALITY OF THE DISTINCTIONS THAT YOU MAKE!

This book aims to provide tools of understanding that will make your communications more harmonious on the personal as well as on the professional plane. These tools are often presented in the form of distinctions between elements which may seem alike but which, in fact, are quite different. Decoding the distinctions between these points will permit you to greatly improve your understanding of life and, consequently, your life itself!

In the preceding chapter, you learned that the quality of your life is directly proportional to the quality of your questions. Now, here is another metabelief of SFC: **The quality of your life is also proportional to the quality of the distinctions that you make**.

From one point of view, **this book** can be considered to be **a series of enriching distinctions**.

You are wondering what I mean by "distinctions"? Let me give you an example. Today, we all know that we react spontaneously in prioritizing one mode of perception rather than another: Some persons react first in a visual way, others in auditory mode and still others kinesthetically, that is to say, they perceive persons, situations, the atmosphere more by their feelings than by sound or sight.

A COUPLE IN DIFFICULTY

As a consultant, I have worked with many couples in difficulty. I knew a man who was auditory and who used to say to his wife "I love you." And he wanted to hear those same words. His spouse was kinesthetic. She gave hugs and wanted to receive hugs. They were on the verge of divorce when they came to my office.

I explained these distinctions (visual, auditory, kinesthetic) and the person who was auditory learned to make the tender little gestures the other was waiting for. The other who was kinesthetic learned to say "I love you." They lived happily and had many children. Do you understand better, now, the importance of distinctions?

This example is, of course, an exaggerated simplification, but it gives a good picture of **the distinctions which can enrich our lives**.

In the second chapter, we have already explained an extremely **important distinction** among the three generations of communication. In the third chapter, we noticed how the recognition of the distinctions between these three generations affects the style and the quality of your questions. If you belong to the first generation, for example, many of your questions will begin with the word "why." The explanation of problems with reference to the past will be of great interest to you. If you favor the third generation, you will prefer to ask solution focused questions and you will move more rapidly toward the "energizing" of solutions in the future. First, second, third generation: **enriching distinctions!**

Throughout this book, we will present you with **other enriching distinctions**. Among the most important, I wish to **emphasize** the three styles of cooperation (chapter 6) and the three types of animals in the sea (chapter 12).

SFC has a pleasantly surprising simplicity. Let us look now at its **three elementary rules**.

Chapter 5

THE THREE ELEMENTARY RULES

THE PRINCIPLE OF OCCAM'S RAZOR

Have you ever noticed how often we human beings are geniuses at complicating our lives? Perhaps you have already heard of the principle of Occam's razor. Guillaume d'Occam is considered to be one of the greatest thinkers of the Middle Ages. He used to say, **"If there are several solutions, always choose the simplest one!"**

Among the characteristics of Solution Focused Communication which attracted me, one of its most pleasing was its **simplicity**. The first generation is quite complex; one can work for years before truly mastering it. The second generation is less complicated, but it is an approach based on expertise that can also take a long time to integrate. The third generation, on the other hand, is extremely simple. Often after their first contact with this philosophy, students begin to apply it with success.

In Solution Focused Communication, there are three simple rules that we call "the elementary rules."

RULE NUMBER 1: IF IT WORKS, DON'T CHANGE IT!

Often, we change what works or we even invent problems. We cultivate the art of complicating things. Before the consultant arrives on the scene the problem is relatively simple, but when he leaves, either he has discovered several more problems, or, again, because of its being studied, the problem has become bigger. This is what we call "the hypothesis of the tip of the iceberg."

RULE NUMBER 2: AS SOON AS YOU KNOW WHAT IS WORKING, WHAT IS GOING WELL, DO MORE OF WHAT WORKS!

The idea here is that in our businesses, in our government offices, in our schools, in our families, there are many things that are going well for the persons in difficulty. When we discover that, it becomes interesting to **water the flowers...not the weeds**. It becomes interesting to emphasize what works, what is doing well!

THE EXCEPTION-QUESTION

In the approach set forth in this book, our first key question is the miracle-question (chapter 3). The second is the **exception question**. It helps us **to uncover and to identify the resource states** and the **current (already present) solutions** of our relatives, of our clients or of our fellow workers. We can find them immediately after having determined the goal to reach for.

First, we use the miracle-question to discover the primary goal with the key words of the other person.

THE STORY OF THE HANDICAPPED CHILD

A couple have a handicapped child. Before the birth of this child, the man and the woman were very successful on a professional plane. They lived in a lovely house in a wealthy neighborhood and they were surrounded by interesting friends. Without a doubt, the arrival of the child upset their life. To discover at the time of birth that one has a child with serious problems is very difficult. It is hard to accept.

The miracle-question permitted us to identify the key words of these parents who found themselves at an impasse: If things were going better, peacefully, in this stressful situation, what would be different?

The father said: "I would be **more relaxed** at home."

And the mother: "I would **accept** my child's problem **better!**"

There are the **key words** of these people, of this couple.

Often, without intending to, we impose our key words on those in difficulty around us. But with this approach, with the miracle-question, we have the key words of the other person revealed to us.

We have found that the father has a need to be **more relaxed** and that the mother feels a need to **better accept** the situation.

When we discover the key words of the other person, we can move on to the exception-question.

THE EXCEPTION-QUESTION

"**Are there already times** [exceptions] **when you** are a little **more relaxed** at home [the father's goal]?"

"Are there already times [exceptions] **when you accept** the situation of your child [the mother's goal] **a little more?**"

We now know what the problem is. In order to have a more complete **picture**, we need information on what takes place **when** the problem is not there.

When are you not so aware of the problem?" "When do you experience the problem **less**?" These are possible formulations of the exception-question. Notice particularly the importance here of the adverb "when." This word serves the purpose of building a **hypnotic presupposition**. We are, in effect, **speaking indirectly to the unconscious mind** of the parents. And the message presupposed by the word "when" is the following:

There are already moments when things go better...or **a little less badly!**

Now, we are going to **water these exceptions; we will emphasize the times when things are better**

This is not at all a denial; it is the amplification, the validating of real, current solutions.

The hypnotic presupposition is the subtlety of this approach. We are no longer speaking directly to the other, we are addressing his unconscious mind where the resources, the solutions are. It is very efficient and very respectful!

You are not engaged in making the other guilty, of blaming him or of convincing him of anything. You are placing your attention on his resources, on his full potential.

**You are discovering, you are locating a flower
which can be watered!**

Note carefully that if you are dealing with a person who is a super-Complainant, a person who says to you: "It is disgusting! It is appalling...it is dreadful...it is unbearable, nothing is working in my life," you cannot say "Are there times when things go well?" It is better to relax, to ask the question in a way that relates to **the current truth** of the other person. Consequently, the question will be worded a little differently.

THE STORY OF THE COMPLAINING MOTHER

An associate told me that after she had discovered this approach, her relationship with her mother was transformed. This friend is very positive, but her mother constantly lamented her lot in life. In the past, her daughter always encouraged her. She attempted to help her to see her life from a positive angle. In an effort to encourage her, she used to speak directly to her and that was not working.

This friend changed her approach with her mother significantly after her discovery of **SFC**.

One day when her mother was complaining anew about her health, this friend used the exception-question which was especially formulated for addressing persons who are Complainants. She asked her simply **"Are there some times when things go a little less badly?"** She was quite astonished to hear her mother reply "Yes, certainly," finally describing some times when things were going better in her life. In reality, it was the same question but asked in a way that respected the **current truth** of the other **(pacing).**

If someone says "It is **depressing**, it is **dreadful**," you can utilize these words with the exception-question "Are there moments when it is **a little bit less depressing, a little bit less dreadful**?" Or even "**When** are things a little bit less bad?"

This is Ericksonian hypnosis. The word "**when**" and the key words of the person in distress permit you to speak indirectly to the unconscious mind of the person.

You remember the story of Milton Erickson's horse? He accompanied the horse into the field of the problems **(pacing)** and very gently, very respectfully, very peacefully, he brought him back to the road of solutions.

In Solution Focused Communication, that is exactly what we do. We accompany the other person into the field of problems, into the valley of tears, and very respectfully, very gently, we lead him back onto the **road of solutions – the road of exceptions –** of unsuspected resources.

A friend who had taken a training on the SFC approach said to me: "Milton Erickson at the age of fifteen on the back of an unknown horse, this is a metaphor which will serve me all my life!"

> **Exploration and explanation of exceptions!**
> **The explanations of problems interest me**
> **less and less!**
> **The explanations of the exceptions to the problem**
> **interest me more and more!**

It is these exceptions to the problem that I am going to validate, to amplify, to **water**. The explanations of the exceptions of my associate, of my partner, of my spouse or of my child are already there; that is what I am going to reinforce.

What is different? When do things go well? How can we explain that the problem is not present at this moment?

Through these messages addressed indirectly to the unconscious, what is **the true message** presented to the person who is depressed, who is full of negative thoughts? The real message is that **there are already times when things are a little bit better** – a little bit less bad – and that these moments, these exceptions, lead us toward potential solutions. **How do we explain these successes**?

Many of our fellow workers, our associates and those close to us do **negative hypnosis,** and they are depressed:

"This is not working! I am at the end of my rope! I can do no more! I am worn out! I am on the verge of collapse!"

With the exception-question, you may **help the other person** to **again find his resources**, his **unsuspected solutions**, **neglected** until now! You can help him abandon his "negative cassette" by means of exceptions that you can discover and search out together.

POSITIVE BLAME

When I was more of a first generation consultant, and when, for a long time, I used to ask clients to explain their problems, it was a form of **negative blame** that I was using. In fact, when the client talked about his problems, he was making himself guilty, he was blaming himself, he was devaluing himself. This took away his energy rather than building it up.

Today, I speak for a shorter time about what is going badly – it is important to listen – but very quickly, after having paced the client (putting oneself in harmony with the other person, respecting his current reality), I leave the field of problems in order **to lead the client back onto the road of solutions.**

It is quite possible that the person in front of you wishes only to complain and is still not ready to take action (a "Complainant"). Your objective then will be to lead him back peacefully and respecfully onto the road of solutions, strengths and good goals. First, you will make use of the miracle-question, which will permit you to determine these objectives. Then you will use exception-questions to search out the solutions that are already there.

When we ask for **explanations of exceptions**, past successes or present solutions, we are beginning to use what we call **"positive blame."**

How were you able to do that?

The true message hidden in this question is **"You have been capable! You are capable! You are capable!"** But we do not say it directly to him. We say it **indirectly**. The true message is **presupposed in the question.**

61

AND WHAT ELSE?

We again ask the question "**And what else? What more?**" This is a refinement, an amplification of the exception-question:

"What explains the fact that **things are going better?**"

"What is it that explains why you were more capable of communicating with your colleague, your associate, your principal fellow worker?"

Again, "What explains the fact that **you have been capable** of moving ahead a little bit more and a little better toward your goal?"

And again, "What explains the fact that **you are capable?**"

You are capable! You are capable! You are capable! You see the game? We blame the person for having succeeded. **We blame him for having been capable**! This technique of exploration and explanation of the exception allows us to **have access to and to elicit the person's success strategies**.

Often people arrive telling us at the same time, both verbally and non-verbally: "I am exhausted, I am a poor passive victim and without resources, I can do nothing!" It is **very important not to contradict** this person unless you have before you what we call "a Customer," that is, a person ready to take action.

We speak indirectly to the unconscious by means of **subtle questions** which **empower the other person**.

As a good cheerleader, we are going to unearth solutions. We are going to ask the miracle-question and exception-questions to discover how to attain the primary objectives.

SOLUTION FOCUSED TASKS

Another way of identifying the exceptions (possible solutions) and of helping the person to **do more of what works** (rule number 2) is to assign solution focused tasks. There are three of them that I want to talk about. The first is the following:

OBSERVE...CONTINUE!

Task 1: "Between now and your next visit, observe what is taking place in your life (family, work, etc.) that you wish to have continue."

This task is very vague, soft, gentle and, especially, **non threatening**. On the conscious level, I have said "Observe what you wish to retain in your life!" But what have I presupposed? **On the unconscious plane**, I have just said "There are already all sorts of things which work in your life. Look for what works and tell me about your exceptions!" I did not say it directly. I said it indirectly!

In effect, the message is "Something valuable is going to happen that you will wish to keep happening." We are giving the person power. We can help him to **undo his negative memories** that are pessimistic and dysfunctional and to **rebuild memories**, **beliefs**, **attitudes** that are more **optimistic, positive, functional**. That is the **solution focused game** and therein lies the subtlety and the efficiency of the solution focused approach. We do not talk directly to everybody, only to "Customers" (persons ready to take action). Most of the people who are difficult to help are those whom we are going to call "Complainants" and "Visitors" (chapter 6). We **speak** to them **indirectly** until they become Customers, to whom we can then speak directly.

OBSERVE...WHEN?

As soon as, through the miracle-question, we have determined a good goal with our employee, our spouse or our child: "I feel better at the plant – I communicate better with my spouse – my results are better at school," we are going to insert these key words into the next task.

Task 2: "Between now and the next time that we meet, **observe** what is happening when you feel better at the plant, **when** you are communicating better with your spouse, when your results are improving at school."

The purpose of this task is to help the person **identify and/or construct exceptions to the problem**. This permits him to capitalize on the times spent in desirable experiences. Again our famous word "**when.**" What is the presupposition implicit in this task? What is the real message?

There are already times when you have strengths, resources, successes, ways to resolve the problem, solutions!

You have not said it to him directly in order not to contradict his conscious mind. On the unconscious plane, the message is "**I know that there are exceptions**, that there are highs and lows in the life of each and every one of us. Each high is an exception!"

As soon as you have discovered and identified some exceptions, you can use the technique of exploration and explanation of the exceptions. Then you can present the third solution focused task.

Task 3: "Keep up your good work. Do more of what works!"

THE SCALING-QUESTION

As soon as the main objective has been determined (ex.: things are going better at the office, at home, with your adolescent), we can work with our third solution focused question: the **scaling-question**.

64

Q: On a scale of 1 to 10 (1 being the lowest level and 10 being the desired state as described through the key words of the client, defined by means of the miracle-question), **where are you situated right now?**

A: Ah! I am only at 2. Things are going badly! Things are very bad!

Q: What would it take for you to go from 2 to 3?

Scales are used to help the person make little movements. The objective is to **find the smallest movement** necessary to help this person.

People often wish to find themselves immediately at 8, 9 or 10 on the scale. As long as they **are resisting** the fact of not being there, they will remain at 2 or 3 (Complainant, passive victim). In order to lessen their resistance, we can say: "Change is like life. There are highs and lows. Instead of making big changes, we move forward through little ones." This "dedramatizes" and diminishes unrealistic expectations.

We make little changes in the right direction. That is encouraging! That is stimulating! We reinforce the little changes. This is a systemic approach in which we seek out little changes.

Q: Where are you now on the scale?

A: I am at 2!

Q: What must happen? What is it going to take for you to progress from 2 to 3 on the scale?

SCALES ARE REMARKABLE IN
IDENTIFYING EXCEPTIONS!

You can also ask someone: "Where were you on the scale of well-being two years ago, one year ago, six months ago, three months ago, one month ago, two weeks ago, one week ago?" Or again: "Where were you on the scale last week? Monday? Tuesday? Wednesday? Thursday? Friday?" etc.

So, you see how the technique works? You see that this recognizes the highs and lows and that **each high** on the scale provides **an exception that we can water and reinforce**.

Complainants are going to put the emphasis on the lows; we are going to listen to the lows. The horse is in the field of problems. And then we are going to **lead the horse** back, very gently, peacefully, respectfully, **onto the road of exceptions**.

But how do you explain that you were you at 7 on the scale two years ago? What was different? How do you explain that things were going better?

With children, you can use a thermometer with color crayons. Colors rather than numbers. A thermometer a day! They learn early that life has highs and lows. And you question...

"How does it happen that you were so high on the thermometer on Monday? What was different for you? And what else? And what else?"

AND WHAT ELSE?

"And what else?" is a powerful intervention! What other element explains why things were going better last Thursday? If you are the guardian or counselor of this young child, you may also ask: "How would your parents explain that things were going well on Thursday?"

We have talked just now about our two main elementary rules:

RULE NUMBER 1:
If it works, don't change it!

RULE NUMBER 2:
As soon as you know what functions, **do more of what works**.

Now we are ready for our third rule.

RULE NUMBER 3:
IF SOMETHING DOES NOT WORK:
• DON'T CONTINUE TO DO IT!
• DO SOMETHING DIFFERENT!

If something is not working, don't do it any longer! This is incredible!

As simple as that! Who would have thought of that? Certainly not the consultants and the communicators of the first generation who think that they possess the truth.

Certainly not the American tourist who was talking more loudly to the Parisian waiter who did not understand English! Certainly not the exhausted mother who screamed harder to maker her difficult child see reason.

When something doesn't work, we human beings have a tendency to fall into vicious circles, to repeat what does not work. We have a tendency to do again what is not going well with our employees, our fellow workers, our associates, with our spouse or with our children.

In the future, as communicators of the third generation, we no longer do what does not work!

The basic belief – **there is not only one solution, there are thousands** – helps us immensely in these difficult situations where we feel caught in the trap, in vicious circles. If I think that there is only one solution (one truth), even if it does not work I am going to continue to insist on trying this sterile choice. However, if I believe that there are thousands of solutions, **I am more ready to abandon** my first attempt at a solution because I know that many other possibilities exist.

The story of the horse reminds us that "there are many paths!" And, as much as possible, **it is the horse who is going to choose the road and the speed.** And when you respect the horse, that works well! It speeds up the walk. But if you are an expert, if you have the truth, believe me, you will experience many conflicts in your life, again and again, on both the professional and personal levels.

When you try something with your principal associate, with a director of services, with your child, and it does not work, **is that a failure? No**...Remember...**it is a learning**! And what is this learning? If it does not work, you have just learned that you need to change **your** thinking and/or **your** way of intervening.

IT IS SIMPLE, BUT NOT OBVIOUS!

Certainly we can fall again and again into vicious circles with our colleagues, our fellow workers, our spouse, our children. We are human beings. We can fall again into the same old traps...like everybody else. But we now have the ability to wake up a little more quickly. Do you like the elementary rules of the solution focused approach?

1. If it works, don't change it!

2. As soon as you know what is functioning, **do more of what works**!

3. If something doesn't work, don't do it anymore! and...

DO SOMETHING DIFFERENT!

Important beliefs:

• There is not just one solution, there are thousands!

• There are no failures, only learnings.

We have just talked about the three elementary rules. We have introduced also the techniques of the exceptions question, the scaling-question as well as solution focused tasks. Let us look now at what many practitioners of SFC consider to be **the jewel of the approach**: **the three styles of cooperation** of the people we are talking to.

Chapter 6

THE THREE STYLES
OF COOPERATION

Have you ever met people who resist you at work, in the family, in your social or private life? On your part, have you ever resisted anyone in the different spheres of your life?

Well, as for me, for fifteen years, I have never been faced with a situation or met anyone who resisted me. You find that interesting? I live in an interesting world, don't you think? Nevertheless, I am not an extraterrestrial!

In this approach, Solution Focused Communication, we believe firmly that **there is no resistance.**

**No matter what the other person does, it is his
unique way of cooperating!**

Before presenting you with the three styles of cooperation, the three unique ways to cooperate, I would like first to tell you another story.

THE STORY OF THE YOUNG SOCIAL WORKER

When I was a young social worker, a family in difficulty came to consult me. One Sunday when the father was riding his bicycle, he had been hit by a truck. The accident had caused a brain concussion, which had serious repercussions for his family and his two children.

At that time, I was more associated with the first and second generation of communication, more based on the expert approach. So I had confidence in direct tasks, and I said to the family "You can do this and that!"

When they came back for the second meeting, they had not completed the tasks that I had assigned. I was disappointed, a little discouraged. But I again gave them the exact same tasks. They returned for the third meeting still without having done them. Again disappointed, I once more gave them things to do. At the fourth meeting, still without result, I was angry. I thought that **they were resisting me**, that **they were not cooperating** with me in their own interest, that they were **not motivated**, that these were truly **difficult people**. Nevertheless, I wished to give them one last chance and so, naturally, I once again assigned tasks for them to accomplish during the week.

You recognize here the American tourist who speaks more loudly in English to the Parisian waiter who does not understand his language? The exhausted mother who screams harder so that her child will finally obey her?

When my clients returned for the fifth meeting telling me that they had not accomplished the tasks, I was truly frustrated and I lost my temper. I told them that I could no longer work with them **because they were resisting me**. I know very well that you have never done that with your relatives, with your clients, even less so with your children.

You have never done what I did before discovering the solution focused approach, have you?

You can keep this story in mind while I am talking about the methods of cooperation. This approach affirms that the word "resistance" does not exist. **No matter what the other does, it is his unique way of cooperating with you!**

Let us see now the three styles of cooperation in the SFC approach. We call the person who adopts the first style of cooperation the "Visitor."

THE VISITOR

What is a Visitor? It is **someone who thinks that there is no problem**. Visitors often go to consult a professional because someone else has sent them: a parent, a judge, a director, an employer, a spouse, etc. Many examples of this type of cooperation come to mind.

In business firms, in offices, these are the people who appear to be there only to receive their pay. If you are a manager, it is important that you recognize that certain of your employees are Visitors.

For example, in a metal production **factory**, during an eight-hour work period, the employees are supposed to pour the metal at regular two-hour intervals. The schedules are well respected during the day but during the night shift, certain employees discovered that they could pour all the product in one period and sleep the rest of the night while being paid $25 to $30 per hour. The result is not totally unacceptable, but it is obvious that the quality of the product is certainly superior when the task is carried out as designed.

73

The supervisors, when they arrive in the morning, take note of the drop in quality. They think that there is a problem. Nevertheless, the employees who have used this strategy are content. They do not see any problem. They are **Visitors**. It is strategically very important that the supervisors recognize the style of cooperation of these people.

When I worked in **the school system** as a social worker, I knew a teacher who was experiencing a great deal of difficulty with one of his students. Not only was Jack not succeeding, but he was constantly disturbing the class. The teacher sent him to the principal, who sent him to me.

When he arrived in my office, I asked him,

"Jack, what is the problem?"

Will you be surprised at his reply?

"I don't have any problem! Everything is going fine!"

Do you understand why we call this style "**Visitor**"?

It is simply someone who does not recognize that there is a problem.

It is easy to give other examples of this behavior. When I was **a marriage counselor**, I often noted that a member of the couple before me was a Visitor. Will I surprise you when I say that generally, it was the man who was the **Visitor**? Indeed, often, the man did not realize that there was a problem.

I also worked with probation officers in **correctional services**. When the prisoner is released, if he wishes to retain his freedom, he must report to a probation officer, once a week, once in two weeks or every month. Do you think that he wants to report to his probation officer?

It is certain that at the beginning, the prisoner, freed conditionally, will be a **Visitor** obliged to present himself. If the probation officer understands and accepts this, he will be astonished at what will happen progressively as the meetings proceed.

I have worked also for **Youth Protection Services**. I noticed that very often, the parents are Visitors. They say: "Yes, I beat my child, but that is how I was brought up. And a good cuff never killed anyone!" Do you see that these parents are **Visitors**? That they do not recognize that there is a problem?

It is very important, whatever your field of activities may be, to recognize Visitors.

When I worked as consultant to **Employment and Immigration Service** of Canada, a job-search program had been initiated for women who were receiving a social welfare allowance. When a woman registered in this course, her allowance was increased. Do you think that all these women wished to return to the workplace? All were **Customers** for the increase of the allowance, but certainly a number among them were, in the beginning, **Visitors** for the teaching contained in this program.

The poor teachers were collapsing under the effort required to treat everybody as Customers (someone who is ready to take action). Many teachers were on the point of suffering professional burnout. They were giving tasks. They had exceptional expectations, believing that everyone was planning to return as quickly as possible to the workforce.

It you are a teacher at a secondary or even at a primary level, the **Visitor** is the student who always arrives late, who looks at the ceiling, who throws gum to distract the other students. It is very important to recognize that you have Visitors in your class in order to **better cooperate** with them.

In the past these people were labeled as lacking in motivation, willingness and desire to cooperate. Such labels are **negative reframes** which are communicated to persons sensitive to non-verbal communication, **harming the relationship** of cooperation that we wish to establish with that person (pupil, associate, fellow worker, etc).

As I perceive it, we all possess **telepathic faculties** and we know everything about the other person, at least **on the unconscious level**. When someone gets on your nerves, do you think that he does not know it? **The non-verbal speaks very loudly!**

On the other hand, when you like and **accept** someone, when you respect your office colleague, your client, he feels that too.

Do you remember the story of the horse? Did you notice the **respect** that Milton Erickson displayed for the horse? The gentleness with which he approached him? I have already mentioned that we have **three primary metaphors** in SFC. The first is **"I do not have the truth!"** That is a very important key! The second metaphor, **the story of the horse**, expresses the respect, the acceptance and the peace which underlie **this approach of cooperation.**

It is very important to manage your inner being, to treat yourself constantly as **the principal person you can help** because the other will receive your telepathic communications. Check how you feel, question yourself as to whether the other person is **resistant, negative, not motivated,** or if you see him instead as a **Visitor who has a unique way of cooperating?** Do you feel the difference in energy between the two ways of perceiving the other person?

Instead of fighting someone energetically, verbally or even non-verbally, you can begin to feel **more peace and acceptance** by using the distinctions of the three styles of cooperation. Do you remember the Serenity Prayer? Call on the serenity in yourself. The other person will feel it, in turn, and find unsuspected resources and solutions which will astonish you.

A Visitor, on the conscious plane, has neither the expectation nor the desire to change. Many people whom you perceive as difficult belong in this category.

Strategically, whatever your field of activity may be, it is important to manage your time well and to **recognize the style of cooperation** that you can expect from the person who is in front of you.

WHAT DO WE DO WITH VISITORS?

I am going to outline some potential strategies for working with Visitors. As surprising as this may appear, we are looking for **strengths** and the **positive characteristics** within these people. We give Visitors **positive feedback**. Instead of being disappointed by their behavior, we find what we can appreciate in them. It is very interesting to realize that we are no longer creating resistance on the energetic plane. On the contrary, by our new attitude we will be contributing to the circulation of energy. What else are we going to do with Visitors?

SLOW DOWN TO SPEED UP!
SPEAK INDIRECTLY TO THE UNCONSCIOUS!

Let us again take the example of Jack, the fifteen-year-old adolescent who was constantly disturbing his mathematics teacher. His teacher sent him to the principal of the school, who then sent him to the solution focused consultant.

"Good-morning, Jack. What is the problem?"

"There is no problem!"

Does the communicator experience a failure? No, it is simply a learning. And what has he learned? That he has a Visitor in front of him. He knows how to cooperate with this type of person. He will not try to convince Jack, nor speak directly to his conscious mind. He is going to slow down in order to speed up: He will **pace** his client. In Ericksonian hypnosis, pacing means that we are **going to slow down** to enter into the world of the other. We are going to build **a relationship of cooperation** with the other person.

"Jack, what are you doing at school? What is your favorite course?"

"Physical Education!"

"And what else?"

"I play on the hockey team."

"What is your position? Oh! you scored a goal recently? What do you do outside of school? Ah! you have a girlfriend? Do you invite her to the movies? And what else? Ah! you work at McDonald's? How many hours a week? How much do you earn? What do you do with your money?"

When you have used the time allotted to Jack, establishing rapport, you thank him for coming.

He might ask you if he could come back to see you.

"But why, Jack, since there isn't any problem?"

"Yes, but this mathematics teacher, he is very exasperated by my way of behaving and he is getting on my nerves."

Have you noticed that **the Visitor has become a Complainant**? He has suddenly changed categories. He recognizes that there is a problem.

This is one way of proceeding with a Visitor. Certainly, this story is a metaphor which can be applied as much to your fellowworker, your associate or your child as to your student.

THE COMPLAINANT

What is **a Complainant**? It is **a person who recognizes that he has a problem**, but **does not yet feel able to do anything** about it. This is someone who appears in your life, saying:

This is dreadful! It is unbearable. I have a very big problem. I am suffering...and I continue to suffer.

And, with the best intentions in the world, you say: "Perhaps you could try to do this! Or that!"

And the Complainant invariably replies:

"But you know perfectly well that I cannot do this because...and I can't do that either. Yes, but, I cannot...! Yes, but.... Yes, but.... Yes, but...."

Often, we call Complainants communicator killers! Manager killers! Parent killers! Teacher killers! We recognize them by their vocabulary. They frequently say: "Yes, but...."

A COMPLAINANT IS A PERSON WHO HAS A PROBLEM BUT WHO DOES NOT YET FEEL THE DESIRE TO TAKE ACTION!

Just as we have understood that we do not have the truth, so we can also recognize that **the current truth of a Complainant** is that he is a **poor passive Victim** who can do nothing. On the conscious plane, the Complainant says to himself: "I have nothing, I have no resources. I can't do anything!"

It is very important for us to **recognize** and **respect his unique way of cooperating**. For the moment, the style of cooperation of this person expresses itself in Complainant mode.

In the past, the Complainant was labeled as **"resistant,"** **"not motivated"** or, again, **"non-cooperative,"** all of which are certainly negative reframes. And even if they are not expressed, negative reframings are felt telepathically by the other person.

In Solution Focused Communication, we know that negative reframes damage or hinder the relationship of cooperation that we wish to develop. With this approach, we avoid such conflicts.

WHAT DO WE DO WITH COMPLAINANTS?

We assign them **observation tasks** (see chapter 5) in order to uncover the exceptions, but, above all, we give no action tasks. That is totally contraindicated! That would discourage them because in so doing, you would be contradicting their present truth! Their conscious tape repeats to them: "I am a poor passive victim. I can do nothing!" If you ask them to do something, you are going to compromise the relationship of cooperation. It is time to...

SLOW DOWN TO SPEED UP!

With a Complainant, we are going to use **exception-questions** (with the Complainant formulation) so as to identify his strengths, his resources, his potential solutions.

"Are there times already, my dear, when things are **a little bit less bad?"**

As soon as you have found the exception, you can use the technique of **exploration** and **explanation of the exceptions** (see chapter 5).

POSITIVE BLAME

You can blame the Complainant. Blame him for having succeeded. Blame him positively.

"How is it that you succeeded last week? How do you explain that you succeeded in that mathematics examination, Jack? What was different?"

These are some examples of **messages addressed indirectly to the unconscious** mind with a solution focused exception-question.

You can also use **scaling-questions** to discover **the highs** and **the lows** in the person's life. Naturally, each experience of a "high" (or each less bad "low") can be conceived of and used as an exception.

THE CUSTOMER

Finally, we arrive at the most delightful communication style for all communicators, for employers, for parents, for managers: the Customer.

What is a Customer? It is a **person who knows that he has a problem** and who is **ready to do something** to transform it or to manage it. Someone who is ready to create solutions.

To the Customer, we can give **direct tasks**. You can have confidence that the employee, the partner, the assistant, the adolescent, the spouse will accept the task and will find it useful.

Have you ever had a problem with a person of the type that we are calling a Customer? No, they are easy to deal with.

It is the **Visitors** and the **Complainants** with whom you experience **difficulty**, is it not?

Do you understand that outside one's professional life, our parents, our spouse, our children can sometimes be Visitors, Complainants or Customers? **These categories of cooperation**, these styles, are **in a state of flux.** No category is fixed in stone once and for all. **The categories vary, changing even in the course of the same conversation.**

HIGH SPEED
MEDIUM SPEED
LOW SPEED!

Several months after a three-day seminar that I had given on the North Shore in Quebec, Canada, one participant said to me:

"We don't much like the terms 'Visitor', 'Complainant' and 'Customer.' We changed them in the following manner: we call the **Customers** people of **high speed**, the **Complainants** people of **medium speed**, and the **Visitors** people of **low** or **slow speed**."

It was truly the unconscious mind of that employee that was speaking because those who are familiar with this area (the North Shore) know that among themselves, the people who live there identify their region by the terms High North Shore, Medium North Shore and Lower North Shore; hence the designations, high speed, medium speed or low speed.

One manager told me that he had very much appreciated this way of perceiving his fellowworkers, his colleagues, his employees, his clients (his Visitors, Complainants and Customers). The idea that there were people around him who operated at **three different speeds** permitted him to adapt well to these three significantly different realities (truths). "You know, Fletcher, there is not only my speed. I adapt myself now to the speed of others. That is fruitful and it is truly **good for business!**"

Another man told me one day: "This approach works very well with the majority of my employees. But it doesn't work at all with one member of my team. He is experiencing a big problem. To help him, I ask:

'What can you **do** to improve the situation, to put the problem in order?' But this does not work at all with him."

As a consultant, the first question that I would ask this manager who is experiencing difficulty with his department head is:

"Are you talking to a Visitor, a Complainant or a Customer?"

"This is a super-Complainant that I have in front of me!"

"In SFC, do we employ the word **'do'** with a Complainant?"

He understood.

To a Customer, we can ask the question directly: "What can you do?"

But the word **"do"** is **totally contraindicated** for Complainants and Visitors. We must use a very different language for each style of cooperation. And we need to **adjust our language** to provide **better pacing** so that we may more effectively enter into the current truth of the other person.

Most of us have a tendency to always think of people as Customers. The **key word** for **Customers** is **do**. But it is necessary to respect the reality of Complainants and Visitors. Once more, we must **slow down in order to speed up**.

A better formulation for Complainants is: **"What must take place?"** Or, again, **"What needs to happen to improve the situation?"**

For "a poor passive victim," we use **passive language**: What must take place? It is not the poor victim who must do something, but the poor victim will show you what needs to be done. You are **speaking indirectly** to **the unconscious mind** of the person, the place where the resources, the solutions are to be found.

OBSERVATION TASKS FOR COMPLAINANTS!

To Complainants, we assign observation tasks. For example, observe...continue...(see chapter 5). What is happening that you want to have continue to happen? To Customers, we can give both observation tasks and action tasks.

If you cannot tell which category the other person is in, it is **always better to go a little more slowly than to go too fast**. Therefore, if you are not sure if your client is a Visitor (slow speed) or a Complainant (medium speed), it is better to identify him as a Visitor for the moment.

If you are hesitating between the Complainant and Customer styles, choose the method of communication that we use with the Complainant. It is better to go more slowly rather than too quickly so as not to harm the relationship of cooperation that you are building.

Many organizations have reported that the application of **SFC**, with its distinctions between the three types of cooperation (Visitor, Complainant and Customer) and its key motto "**Slow down to speed up**," has proven to be **very profitable** in **both the medium and the long-term**. A team captain who works in a large firm related: "If I had known these distinctions previously, I would not have had to discipline and even suspend certain Visitor-style employees. And, as a result, **I would not have the difficulties that I am now experiencing with the union!**"

84

PREVENTION OF PROFESSIONAL BURNOUT

Many people, in our modern societies, treat everyone as Customers. This completely spoils the relationship of cooperation that we would like to develop with as many people as possible.

The majority among us have been trained to **expect** each person to be a Customer for our management, for our teaching, for our counseling, and **even to demand** that he be a Customer. That's where the difficulty comes in! When we are confronted with Visitors and Complainants, they appear to resist us because we do not respect their current truth and speed. So, we are often disappointed, frustrated, discouraged or even irritated. I am convinced that if we could change this way of seeing things, **the statistics of professional burnout** would **decrease significantly.**

It is important to establish that **the style of cooperation** of the person facing you **can change** in the course of the same conversation. At one moment, this person may be a Customer for what you are saying. The instant after, he could become a Visitor. A little later, he may become a Complainant. And still later, he may again become a Customer.

Your responsibility as a solution focused communicator is to pace him and thus **to speed up and slow down** when it is appropriate.

Too often, we impose our speed on the other person. Remember the story of the horse and the respect that Milton Erickson displayed with regard to this horse. Gently, peacefully and respectfully, he led the horse back onto the road of solutions.

THE STORY OF A SOLUTION FOCUSED MOTHER!

If you ask children if they want to go buy ice cream, in which category will they be? Will they be Visitors? Complainants?

Certainly the chances are great that they will be Customers at that moment. If it is 8 p.m. and you ask your children to go to bed, the chances are strong that they will not be Customers. They are going to look more like **Visitors** or **Complainants**. The solution will be to **speak indirectly to their unconscious mind.**

My sister, Helen, is a solution focused mother and spouse. She applied this philosophy with her two children, Shaun (four years) and Kaylyn (six years). She said to them: "My dear children, would you like to go to bed in five minutes or ten minutes?" This is Ericksonian hypnosis. My sister, Helen, has just addressed a **hypnotic presupposition** to her children. Her real message, underneath, is: "My dear children, you will be in bed no later than ten minutes from now!"

No strategy will work with everyone all the time. And even children, who are very brilliant, will soon catch on to their parents' new method of communication. Some time after Helen adopted this approach, my nephew, Shaun, shouted to his mother, "Mom, are you going to buy me one or two ice creams?"

CONCLUSION

To close the loop, let us add that in **SFC**, the word "resistance" does not exist. It is not useful. **No matter what the other person does**, as much as possible we are going to perceive his communication as **his unique way of cooperating with us**, whether he be a Visitor, a Complainant or a Customer.

Previously we had a tendency to consider everyone as a Customer, to go at high speed. We are predisposed to go too directly, too quickly, with a great many people in our life. Now, we are learning to **slow down to speed up**. And, especially, we are learning to do more **pacing** with our Visitors and Complainants.

We have already spoken about the importance of the effects of our beliefs on our experiences. In the next chapter, we will come back to this theme in order to see how we **create our own reality.**

Chapter 7

YOU CREATE
YOUR OWN REALITY

Presuppositions
+
Basic beliefs
+
Expectations

EXPERIENCE OF "REALITY"
(Self-fulfilling Prophecies)

Our presuppositions and our beliefs create our expectations.
Together, they are going to create our experience
of "reality."

I have put the word "reality" in quotation marks in order to underline the fact that there are several realities and that our perception is often subjective.

If you ask a police officer, he will tell you that when there are a dozen witnesses on the scene of an accident, there are often a dozen significantly different versions of the accident. No one has seen or experienced exactly the same thing as the person next to him did. There are a dozen different ways of perceiving the same reality (the accident).

THE STORY OF THE IQ

A good illustration of the influence of our presuppositions and our beliefs on our experience of the "truth" comes to us from the field of **education**.

In the fifties and sixties in New York, everyone was very impressed by the idea of evaluating the intelligence quotient (the IQ) of students. The danger of these tools is that in using them, one can easily limit the human being.

At that time, at the beginning of each year, the teacher received a list of her students with a number disclosing the intelligence quotient of each beside each name.

A researcher who must have had a peculiar sense of humor, a man named Rosenthal, had the idea of partially falsifying the results of the IQ tests which he felt locked the students into a measure of intelligence that was supposed to be exact and definitive. This researcher took the list of students which he would have to give to the teachers at the beginning of the scholastic year and secretly reversed the results. He lowered the scores of those who had a very high IQ and raised the IQ scores of those who were labeled less intelligent.

At the end of the year, they had to again give the test to each student. Can you guess the result? Strangely, the students obtained basically the same results that the researcher had falsely attributed to them at the beginning of the year. Those who had been classified as of low intelligence but whose IQ score had been raised obtained higher results. And those who had obtained the higher results originally (but whose IQ Rosenthal had lowered for the purposes of the experiment) had lower scores. This is a fine example of what we call **a "self-fulfilling prophecy."**

This example demonstrates very well the effect of our beliefs, of our presuppositions, of our expectations, on another person.

I work with a student; I try to teach him a difficult subject and it does not work. I look at his result on the intelligence test and I see that he has obtained a score of 130(very high). This is a capable, very capable student. I therefore **change my way of intervening with him** so as to awaken the resources that I believe he possesses.

It works! **My beliefs, my presuppositions, my expectations concerning the other person can therefore have a very important effect on my way of perceiving him and on my way of behaving with him. Changes in my beliefs can change my experience of the other person, which, in turn, affects his behavior and his experience.**

THE STORY OF THE PLACEBO: PART ONE

Another story which well illustrates the importance of our beliefs comes from the area of psychosomatic medicine, which evaluates the influence of thoughts on the body. More and more, we recognize that a great many illnesses are generated by causes related to stress.

In the course of a study on pain control, three groups were selected at random from a large number of people who were suffering great pain. To the patients of the first group the research-ers gave morphine, a powerful painkiller, but told them that it acted only as a light pain reliever. To the second group they prescribed a light pain reliever. To the ill people of the third group they supplied only a placebo, that is a sugar pill, which, technically, has no biochemical effect on the body, but the patients were told that it was morphine. The third of the group which received the placebo reported that their pain had entirely disappeared. Not bad for a little sugar pill! The power of thought! The third of the patients who received the real morphine (but who had been told that it acted **only** as a light pain reliever) reported that they were still suffering a lot of pain.

The sugar pill, the placebo labeled as a powerful painkiller, proved more effective than the real morphine labeled as a light pain reliever. You see the importance of thought? On ourselves and on others!

THE STORY OF THE PLACEBO: PART TWO

In a second experiment, the doctors had received instructions to always say the same thing to their clients: "Here is some morphine. It is a powerful painkiller. This is going to help control the pain." However, the doctors did not know, at the time of giving the medication to a patient, if it was the placebo or the morphine.

When the doctors gave the placebo and sincerely believed that it was the real morphine, the pain-relieving effect among the patients increased significantly! But when they gave the real morphine, thinking that it was a placebo, the effect decreased significantly!

Why do I tell this story? Simply to demonstrate that there are **always two levels of communication.** There is the conscious level, and there is the unconscious level. There is the verbal, and the non-verbal. And, according to certain theorists of communication, only **7% of the message is verbal** while **93% of the message comes from the non-verbal.** Even if the verbal message were always the same: "Here is some morphine, a very powerful painkiller that is going to help you control the pain," **the non-verbal message, the inner beliefs** of the doctors, had a very important effect on the experience of their clients. **The non-verbal spoke very loudly**!

Each of us in our own fields is a professional communicator, whether it be in industry, commerce, health care, education or different areas of government. This is why it is important to recognize, to realize that **our principal tool of communication is ourselves: It is our system of beliefs, our attitude, our presuppositions and our expectations**.

CONCLUSION: TWO QUESTIONS

Generally speaking, our goals are the happiness, the satisfaction and the well-being of the people who surround us (both at work and at home) and of the principal person whom we are able to help: ourselves! In the days ahead, I invite you to begin to notice your inner and your outer cassette by asking yourself the two following questions:

Question 1: What does your personal cassette consist of? What are you listening to? What are you saying? What are you seeing?

What are your thoughts? What are your words? And above all, **what are your presuppositions**, what are **your beliefs?**

Question 2: Do not ask yourself if your presuppositions or your beliefs are true, but rather **are they useful for the accomplishment of your goals?**

To review the applications of the tools already contained in this book, here are some questions:

1. Is it more **useful** to have **problems or** to have **opportunities?**

2. Is it more **useful** to undergo **failures or** to experience **learnings?**

3. Is it more **useful** to retain the belief "**I have the truth**...there is **only one solution** (mine)!" **or** to realize that "**I do not have the truth** and **there are thousands of solutions**"?

4. Is it more **useful** to be surrounded, at the office or at home, by **people** who are "**resistant**" or "**not motivated**" (uncooperative) **or** is it more useful to have around you **people who have their unique way of cooperating** (Visitors, Complainants and Customers) that one can identify and respect, and with whom one can more easily cooperate?

We have noticed (chapter 6) that **most of the difficult people in our lives** are those whom we call **Complainants** or **Visitors**. We have recognized also that these persons have a **great many presuppositions, beliefs and expectations that are negative, pessimistic and dysfunctional**.

Our responsibility as a **solution focused communicator** (whether as a manager, spouse, parent, etc.) is to help the people around us to modify these beliefs, these presuppositions and these negative, pessimistic and dysfunctional expectations. We achieve this by using the solution focused techniques presented in the preceding chapters: the questions (miracle, exception, scaling: chapters 3 and 5) and the tasks (observe...do...: chapter 5)

After having read this chapter, you certainly understand the importance of our beliefs and of our presuppositions in influencing and even creating our experience of reality. Now I would like to talk to you a little more about **Milton Erickson**. In the next chapter, we will study his system of thought, **his beliefs** and **his basic presuppositions**.

Chapter 8

ERICKSONIAN PRINCIPLES

Milton Erickson, who was known as the Einstein of communication of the twentieth century, obtained extraordinarily positive results working with the most difficult people.

I wondered, therefore, when I was writing my thesis, "What were **the basic beliefs**, the presuppositions of this genius of communication?"

GROWTH MODEL

I noticed, among other things, that in one metaphor he described human beings as plants or flowers. He used to say, "A plant or a flower can be injured or hurt, but there is always a tendency toward transformation, toward healing, toward growth."

Thus, he always put **the accent on the positive tendencies**, on what works for the person, the human being: on the exceptions, the resources, the solutions which were already there. According to Erickson, if you concentrate your attention on what there is that is positive in the other person, this will create **a great deal more cooperation.**

As a communicator, he cooperated with his clients by not focusing on their conflictual parts but instead by placing the accent on the strengths of the individual. This is again the distinction between the first and the third generation.

> **It is always easier to build with strengths and past successes (the exceptions) than to try to correct mistakes and past failures.**

The first generation tended to correct the pathology while the third generation, oriented toward solutions, is interested in solutions, resources, exceptions and strengths.

WHAT IS THE "OK-NESS PRINCIPLE"?

Milton Erickson said "As awful as the past may have been, tomorrow is another day."

In my work as a consultant, I have seen many horrible things: marital violence, child abuse, attempted murder or suicide. I do not doubt that you have also seen difficult things. It is not always easy to see signs of "OK-ness." According to one of my colleagues in Chicago, John Walter, the solution focused approach is a form of "incurable optimism." There is always hope! It is the principle of "it is OK" or "it is all right" which maintains that behind the difficulties, something is right, there is light. Oh yes, tomorrow is very much and indeed another day!

THE OTHER PERSON ALREADY POSSESSES
THE RESOURCES THAT HE NEEDS

To begin with, we need a realistic goal, an appropriate goal. This can be determined by the miracle-question. Of course, it is necessary to define the criteria of a good goal!

What are they?

First: Is it doable?
Second: Is it doable in the short term?
Third: Can this goal be set in motion (initiated) by
the person in difficulty?

As soon as a good goal has been determined, we believe firmly that **the other person has the resources to attain it**. Recall the research carried out on the IQ. The pupils who were supposed to be less endowed finished the year higher on the scale because the test results had been reversed and the professors **believed** that they were teaching capable students.

If we believe that the person is capable, this increases his chances of showing himself capable and therefore of attaining his goal. This presupposition is just as valuable for the manager with whom you are associated in a project as for your employees, your spouse or your child.

The other person is making the best choice
possible!
Behind all behavior there is a
positive intention!

There are some dreadful, even criminal behaviors. We cannot accept violence toward women or toward children. However, behind each act there is **a positive intention**. We can make a distinction between the behavior and the intention. For example, it is quite possible that the child who disturbs the class at school wishes to attract attention, to be liked. Is this not so?

THE STORY OF THE TROUBLESOME PUPIL

A teacher at the primary level told me that one of her pupils was constantly disturbing the class and that each time the child was clowning about, she endeavored to correct him.

Here is her story: "After the **Solution Focused Communication** training, I realized that Peter's negative behavior revealed a positive intention (he wished to attract attention); therefore I could act in a much more skillful, more appropriate manner with him. I understood that in trying to correct him, I was reinforcing his negative behavior. I was **watering the weeds** (the problem)! I changed my attitude! I began to pay attention to him when he was doing something good, when he was attentive to a dictation or when he was participating appropriately in a group activity. Each time that there was **an exception** in his behavior, I noticed and complimented him to show that I appreciated his attitude. At first he was a little confused but, over time, his harmful acts gradually disappeared because they were no longer useful in his quest for attention."

This teacher's story illustrates very well the metaphor of Solution Focused Communication:

WATER THE FLOWERS...AND OFTEN THE WEEDS
WILL DISAPPEAR FROM LACK OF ATTENTION!

This is **positive hypnosis**. It is putting the accent on what is functioning at work, with employees, in the family. It means finding good goals with the miracle-question, looking for exceptions and using scaling-questions.

Often when we attack a problem, we magnify it, we "guilt" the other person, we blame him, or devalue him. It is important to be aware that each behavior hides a **positive intention** (however unskillfully expressed) and also that the person concerned is making **the best choice possible** for him at the time.

If we look carefully around us, we notice that it is quite exceptional for anyone to try deliberately to do badly. It can happen occasionally that an employee or a child feels helpless, without resources. Our task is to find and reinforce the choice of these people to transform a positive intention into reality, helping them to engage in more appropriate behavior.

I am going to tell you a somewhat controversial story that was reported to me by a social worker dealing with families in difficulty.

"I met a mother who had placed the hand of her child on the ring of a hot stove. Of course that is dreadful and unacceptable! But that woman had a **positive intention**: she wanted to have her son learn not to touch the burner when it was hot. It is certainly not brilliant, but she made **the best choice available to her** in this case. Because I understood her positive intention, I could suggest other ways of teaching the child. The result is that she has never burned either this child or the other younger ones."

Most persons in difficulty do not have many choices at the conscious level. They feel helpless. Our task, as solution focused communicators, is to discover their positive intention. When we know this, we can multiply the solutions at their disposal so that they can make a better choice in order to accomplish their positive intention!

CHANGE IS NOT ONLY POSSIBLE, IT IS INEVITABLE!

Many people around us, at work as well as at home, make what we call "negative generalizations": "Nothing works in my life. Everything is going badly! This employee is making everybody miserable! That team member is dishonest! This will never change!" And so on and so on.

But we discover, on looking carefully at the situation, that there are **highs and lows** in the life of every person. And each high is what we call an **"exception"** that we can uncover and then amplify and water. And we can do this, even if the other person in a given situation affirms, "There is no exception in my work or in my life!" Your gift to that person is to know that there are exceptions!

There are always good days and less good days. Ask the nurses in the hospitals; they will confirm for you that for all patients, there are some good hours and some less good hours in the course of the day.

One nurse who is solution focused asks the **scaling-question** to her patients: "Where were you on the scale of well-being this morning? This afternoon? In the middle of the afternoon? On a scale of 1 to 10, where were you early this evening? And now?" There are highs and lows, and they vary even from one day to the other.

If you ask the **Complainant a scaling-question** of well-being, where will he focus his attention on the scale?

On the high or on the low? On the low, of course! Is he "resisting"? Trying to make you fail? No, this is his unique way of cooperating with us (the Complainant style).

Everyone has **his unique way of cooperating**. People cooperate in the manner of a Visitor, a Complainant or a Customer. Recognizing these distinctions permits you to **better accept each person** and therefore to better deal with every situation and, accordingly, to better move through it.

Now that we are familiar with the basic ideas of Solution Focused Communication, you listen to the horse, you follow him into the field of problems (pacing) and gently, peacefully, respectfully, you lead him back onto the road of solutions – the road of strengths, resources, exceptions and good goals.

We know that there are **good days and less good days**. That there are good weeks and less good weeks. Our work consists in pacing, listening to the lows, then leading the horse back onto the highs.

AN UNDERSTANDING OF THE PROBLEM IS NOT ABSOLUTELY NECESSARY TO OBTAIN CHANGES!

Here, Erickson gives us **a third generation** point of view. In the first generation, we believed that it was absolutely necessary to understand the problem in order to resolve it. Sometimes we spent years in the field of problems. I am not saying that it is completely useless to understand the problem. At work, I sometimes need precise data especially if it concerns technical matters.

But in **Solution Focused Communication**, we spend **less time in the sphere of explanation of the problem**. We go a great deal more rapidly toward the reality that we wish to create and the way of attaining the goal. We ask ourselves what the little steps are that we can take to move toward the realistic goal that has been established. We are looking for what we can accomplish in the short term to move toward this goal. **The focus is on solutions**, not on the explanation of problems.

We have already talked about the importance of our thoughts, our beliefs and our presuppositions. If we help someone to change his thoughts, his beliefs, his presuppositions, this will create changes in his behavior and his emotions (see diagram).

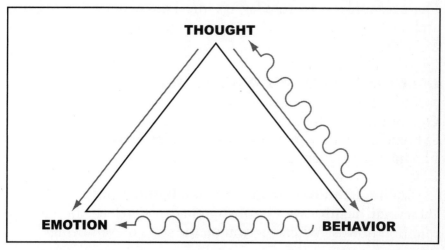

ASK THE CLIENT TO DO SOMETHING!

Our interventions are subtle and often indirect because they are addressed to the unconscious mind. The result of this type of intervention in the **SFC** approach is that behaviors begin to change.

Further, we can help the client to **take action**, to **behave in a different way**.

Simply posing the **miracle-question**, having someone talk about the solution that he envisages, is already watering the flowers, **helping him move**. With the miracle-question (chapter 3), we are asking the client to talk about his desired **goal**, the ideal situation that he wishes to attain.

The act of describing in detail a future in which the problem is already solved helps to create the **expectation** that the problem will be settled. This expectation, once created, can help the client to **think** and to **act** in a way that will lead him to its fulfillment.

The simple fact of posing the **exception-question** leads people to **do** a little **more of what is functioning**. When they change their behavior and are doing more of what works, this creates changes in their thoughts: "Hold it! I am capable. I have strengths! I have resources! Last Tuesday, it's true, I did better. I did this, that and that." This also creates changes in their emotional state. They feel better.

ONLY A LITTLE CHANGE IS NECESSARY!

One of the attractive aspects of the second and third generation approaches is that they are **minimal approaches**. We are not looking for big changes.

Scaling-questions permit the identification of little changes. In several health care establishments in Quebec, the favorite question now is "Where are you on the scale of well-being?"

"I am at 2."

"What would it take to go to 2.1?"

At school, if a student has three good answers in a test containing five questions, it is important to slow down and validate the effort: "You have succeeded in getting three correct responses."

We slow down in order **to increase the self-esteem** of the pupil, to pace him, to reinforce the positive action. And then we can ask "What is it going to take for you to get four or five good answers the next time?" You understand the technique? **Slow down to build up**, to celebrate and reinforce the little changes. We are going to minimize and undo unrealistic expectations. Most people wish to be at 8, 9 or 10 on the scale, and right now! If someone is at a 2, my wish is to help him to get himself to 2.1 or 2.5. I want to help him celebrate this small victory. I am going to value the 0.1 obtained. If someone is at 0, my goal is to help him to get to 0.1. If someone is at -5, my objective is to help him to climb the scale to -4. **Only a little change**. But a change that bears fruit.

In a factory where I was a consultant, the morale of an entire work team was at 2. In five months, thanks to a system of scales, the morale rose to 3, then to 3.5, then 4.7, 5.1 and 6.7. The last time that I met them, they were at 7.5. They made small movements in order to climb the scale.

We have already seen several important Ericksonian principles. In the next chapter, we will go a little more deeply into the theme of **cooperation** and we will study in some detail **the heart of all effective communications**, that is, **pacing and leading**.

Chapter 9

COOPERATION

In the preceding chapters, we saw that the third generation of communication led us directly to a philosophy of cooperation. We accept and use the current reality of our primary associates, of our spouse and of our children.

PACING AND LEADING

Henceforth, we possess tools that enable us to better cooperate, notably **pacing,** which means entering into the world of the other person, joining each person in his world. We accept what the other has to offer, we speak his language, we look for his key words, his sentences, his values, his metaphors.

We saw also that one of the best ways of pacing was to recognize Visitors, Complainants and Customers.

With **Customers**, we can go at **high speed**. No need to slow down, to accompany the horse into the field of problems. No need to do a lot of pacing.

With a **Complainant**, it is necessary to adopt **medium speed**. **We need to slow down**, to do **more pacing**, to go with the horse into the field of problems. We need to speak a little more about the problems, to listen as the other shares them with us.

With a **Visitor**, we must choose **slow speed**. It is necessary to slow down still more, to **do even more pacing** in order to build the relationship. In general, as Visitors see it, it is the others who have problems.

Pacing and leading are tools for all **effective communications**. The word "pacing" means that we are synchronized with someone. The word "leading" indicates what we do when we guide the other person.

**"Resistance" indicates a need
for more pacing.**

Our horse strays into the field of problems. You listen to him, then respectfully, peacefully, you try to lead him back. If the horse protests, is he resisting? Is this a failure? No, it is a learning! And what have you just learned? That it is necessary to slow down and do more pacing with the Complainant horse. The apparent **"resistance"** of this person shows us that there is a **need for more pacing.**

THE STORY OF JESUS CHRIST

A good way of further illustrating pacing and leading is to relate another story from the life of Milton Erickson.

At one time, Milton Erickson arrived at a psychiatric hospital where one patient, John Smith, considered himself to be Jesus Christ. Labeled as a heavy case, John Smith had lived in this institution for ten years. This was a desperate case which had defeated the entire personnel of the hospital.

John Smith was referred to as a **"heavy case,"** a **"difficult case,"** a **"hopeless case."** All the adjectives that were being used to describe the "John Smith case" were **negative reframes** which were not conducive to helping him. They were what, in this book, we would call **"self-fulfilling prophecies."**

Erickson arrived in this institution where, for ten years, all the psychiatrists, nurses, psychologists, officials and social workers had tried to convince John Smith that he was not Jesus Christ. Was John Smith a Customer for that idea? No, certainly not! Had this lack of result prevented the staff from **continuing to do what was not working?** No. They believed that they held the truth; that is why they were set upon repeating the strategy that was not working.

Erickson arrived with another way of looking at the patient. He was ready to **pace** him, to enter, at least temporarily, into the world of the other, to speak the language of the other. He said to him, shaking hands: "Good morning, Jesus. My name is Milton."

What happened spontaneously? The other felt accepted.

Milton Erickson continued:

"Jesus, if I am not mistaken, you are very skilled in carpentry. Your father, Joseph, was a good carpenter and you also know this trade, do you not?"

Jesus said:

"Yes, my father, Joseph, was a carpenter. Yes, I am good at woodwork."

Erickson continued:

"Jesus, if I am not mistaken, your reason for being on the planet, the reason you have chosen to be here with us, is to help, to give to us, is it not?"

105

Jesus-John replied:

"Yes, yes, that is true. That is my mission on the planet!"

You recognize the language of pacing that Milton Erickson was using?

"You are Jesus [pacing]. You are a carpenter [pacing]. You have come to help people [pacing]."

Then Erickson moved on to the next stage [leading]:

"It is interesting, Jesus. There is a big renovation project going on in the hospital. Carpenters, tradesmen, are presently working at building shelves in the library. Would you like to help them? [leading]"

And Jesus-John Smith said:

"I am Jesus, I am a carpenter, I like to help people. Yes. I will help the carpenters!"

And for the first time in ten years, John Smith went to do useful work with the men who were renovating the library of the institution.

There is usually a "punch line" in Milton Erickson stories, and that is the case here.

Eight months later, the big renovation project was completed and the team of workers departed with a new colleague whose name was John Smith!

At this point, it is important to remember that all the stories here are metaphors. We all have a Jesus Christ, **a difficult case** in our life (whether it be at work or in private life). This story illustrates very well the Ericksonian principles that we examined together in chapter 8.

REVIEW OF ERICKSONIAN PRINCIPLES

Number 1: **"The OK-ness principle."** Most of the hospital personnel perceived John Smith as a hopeless case, like a plant or a flower that was badly damaged. All the negative and pathological labels that had been imposed on him came from first generation communicators. They were not of a nature likely to encourage the transformation of this person.

On the other hand, Milton Erickson held deeply different beliefs about the human being.

For Milton Erickson, John Smith was a human being, and **something** in him was **inherently good ("it is OK")**. In spite of ten years of fruitless efforts made by all the people who were involved with John Smith, Erickson arrived with the idea that tomorrow is another day.

Number 2: **The person already has the necessary resources** within himself. Indeed, Milton Erickson succeeded in triggering the unsuspected resources that John Smith needed to move on.

Number 3: **The person makes the best choice possible** at the time. John Smith felt he was Jesus. Erickson increased the choices at his disposal. He could keep all the negative labels that had been bestowed on him or go to work with the carpenters. John Smith made a new choice.

Number 4: **Every behavior has a positive intention**. Erickson understood that this man had not chosen the character of Jesus for nothing. He had chosen it because he wished to help people. Erickson used this positive intention.

Number 5: **Change is inevitable**! Everybody thought that John Smith was **a chronic case**, an impossible case which was never going to change. Milton Erickson, an extraordinary communicator, based his intervention on the presupposition that change was inevitable.

Number 6: **An understanding of the problem is not absolutely necessary**.

Erickson did not try to have John Smith understand that he was not Jesus. Everyone else had tried for ten years to convince the patient of this and it had not worked. It was clear that John Smith was **not** at all **a Customer** for that idea at this time. Rather, he was **a Visitor**.

Erickson asked John Smith to **do something different**. He helped him to go to work with the construction workers and that changed his thoughts. Perhaps it became a little more interesting to be John Smith. That changed his emotions. He felt better!

Also it was **only a little change,** and this little change altered a whole system. It is, as we say, the "snowball effect." Erickson completely **accepted the reality, the present truth** of John Smith and **he used it** for the patient's well-being. I very much like this expression: **present truth**. The word "present" reminds us that our perception of reality is very fluid and changeable. If you accept the current truth of the other, you increase the possibility that this truth can change.

TO CONVINCE: A MILITARY METAPHOR

All the employees of an institution tried for ten years to convince a man that he was not Jesus. Do you understand that **if you are trying to convince someone** of something, **you are already lost?**

Probably **you are employing "Customer" language** (high speed, speaking directly to the conscious mind) **with Complainants and Visitors.**

"To convince" is a military metaphor. You are trying to conquer the present truth of the other person with your superior truth. If you struggle against that truth, you are attacking, you are provoking, you are devaluing that truth and thus you lose the attention of the other person. **Resistance leads to persistence**. Our resistance to the present truth of the other leads to the persistence of the problem.

Finally, Erickson joined the other person in his world, in his present truth. He spoke the language of the other, first by **pacing** him **and** then by **leading** him. This is **the heart of all effective communication**.

You are already doing this with your colleagues, with your spouse, with your children. But many of us **speak too directly** and **too quickly** (Customer language) with many people. In order to better cooperate, **we need to learn to slow down**, to **do more pacing**.

We have already talked about the SFC mottos. Let us now examine another key motto of this approach: **Resistance leads to persistence**.

Chapter 10

RESISTANCE LEADS
TO PERSISTENCE

COOPERATION

Non-Resistance

Resistance ➜ ➜ ➜ ➜   Persistence

Acceptance ➜ ➜ ➜ ➜   a) Decrease
                        b) Disappearance

One day on an airplane, a businessman seated beside me asked, "If you had to summarize in one sentence your **Solution Focused Communication** approach, what would that key sentence be?" I immediately replied "**Resistance leads to persistence.**" From one point of view, the entire **SFC** approach is contained in this little sentence. **What you resist is going to persist.**

A RESISTANT EMPLOYEE

To better illustrate the meaning of this basic motto, let me, once again, tell you a typical story.

A client arrives in my office. He shouts: "This is sickening, it is unbearable, I have a huge problem, I can do no more, I am exhausted, I do not know what to do." The client's words are the problem.

In the **solution focused sequence**, we have:

Number 1: the problem.

Number 2: the goal. "If things are going better, what will it be like? [miracle-question]." He gives me his description in his key words. "Ah! yes, **things will go better at the office**, I will be more relaxed in my work [key words]."

And his goal is to move toward that ideal. But he does not begin immediately to go in the desired direction. He begins to push in the opposite direction, to return to the field of problems. He pushes very hard. (Perhaps this is a Complainant, yes, but.... Yes, but....)

At this point, as a communicator, I might say to myself: "Ah! My God! This person is difficult. He is resistant. He is uncooperative, he is not motivated!" These are all our favorite negative terms that we employ when the person does not wish to go in the direction that we suggest to him, when he is not immediately a Customer for our solution, for our truth.

"You said that your goal was this...and this...and you are doing exactly the opposite. You are hindering the whole process! You are sapping my energy! This is very difficult! I am going to be ill!" And we think: "**This person is resisting me**. He is really not cooperating!"

I know that you have never done this with your collaborators, with your associates, with your spouse. Never in your life! But I, in the past, from time to time, had that happen.

Then I discovered **Solution Focused Communication**.

Now, the person arrives in my office and says: "I have a big problem. Things are bad. It is sickening, it is terrible, it is absolutely frightening." So we work together to discover his goal. His goal is to go in a particular direction, but he begins to push very hard in the opposite direction, to go back into the field of the problem. (Complainant: Yes, but.... Yes, but....) Now instead of trying to convince him to go in the right direction, I am ready to accompany him as he goes the opposite way.

"What a good idea [for the moment]," I say to myself, "to go a little way in this direction! [pacing, pacing, pacing)]"

Previously, I would have **attached a negative label** to this person: resistant, uncooperative, non-motivated.

We do this with our children, with our spouses, our colleagues, our clients, members of our family, etc.

A trick question or a key question: In the first version of this story, **was the person resisting me?**

No! A) He was doing his best; B) He had positive intentions; C) He had his unique way of cooperating (Visitor or Complainant); and D) Something was OK.

In the past, from time to time, **I resisted my clients**. I used to push in the opposite direction when they wished to go in a direction opposite to mine. But did my clients cooperate? Not at all! Was that a failure? No! It was **a learning**. And what did I learn? That I needed to think differently and/or act differently. I was pushing in a direction opposite to that of my client, and **my resistance**

led to the persistence of the problems, difficulties and undesirable behavior.

But **if I accept my client**, my collaborator, at least temporarily (pacing, pacing, pacing), with his unique way of cooperating (Complainant, Visitor), then eventually I am going to **establish rapport** with him. Gradually, I can lead the horse back toward his goal, which will better serve both our interests and those of the organization.

Now, let's look again at the story of Jesus Christ. Milton Erickson did not repeat what had not worked for ten years. He did not come in saying, "You are not Jesus." He knew that **resistance leads to persistence!** Erickson arrived, saying: "Good morning, Jesus [**pacing**]. Ah! you are the son of a carpenter [**pacing**]. Ah! you like to help people [**pacing**]. Would you like to help the workers who are renovating the library [**leading**]? Goal accomplishment. **Pacing and leading**, the heart of all effective communication.

Resistance leads to persistence! **Acceptance (pacing) leads to the decrease** or even the disappearance of the core or the heart of the problem. This is why I say that suffering is optional! As I have already said in this book, I do not deny that suffering exists. However, by **learning to resist difficult people and situations less** in our life, we can at least contribute to the decrease of suffering and perhaps even to its disappearance.

PSYCHOLOGICAL JUDO

You have all heard of the martial arts: tai chi, judo, kung fu, etc.? What I am presenting to you now is a form of **psychological judo**. Instead of pushing in the opposite direction, we will go the same way as the other person for the moment.

If the communicator, the manager, the teacher, the associate, anyone, **sees resistance** in the other person, **he cannot see his efforts to cooperate**. If, on the other hand, **the communicator**

looks for the unique way of cooperating (Visitor, Complainant, Customer) of each person, **he cannot see the resistance.**

TAPE FOR DIFFICULT PERSONS

We all have a tendency to resist certain persons or certain situations in our life. But now, we understand that our resistance often leads to the persistence of the difficulties and even to the deterioration of the situation. Therefore, it is important to have at our disposal as many methods as possible to help us to resist these persons and these difficult situations less.

If you are experiencing difficulties with someone or if you are blaming the other person, you might remember the motto, **resistance leads to persistence**, and you could have the following tape, based on Ericksonian principles, playing in your head: A) This difficult person is doing his best; B) He has positive intentions; C) It is his unique way of cooperating (Visitor, Complainant); and D) Something is OK.

This tape can help you to resist the other person less, to calm yourself, to **bring yourself back to a resource state** where you will have access to all your skills and all possible solutions.

And if you are judging yourself, feeling discouraged, blaming yourself, **you can talk to yourself** using the same tape. A) I am doing my best; B) I have positive intentions; C) It is my unique way of working; and D) Something is OK.

THE MOST DIFFICULT PERSON!

Who is **the principal person that you can help**? All the time? **Yourself!** And **who is** often, very often, **the most difficult person** in your life? Once again, it is **yourself!**

It is very important to be as respectful toward yourself as you are with the other people in your life, to accept yourself as you accept them. And often, if you care for yourself, if you accept yourself, that will make the "outer" world much more pleasant.

Our society is still very much "first generation." Also, if we observe carefully, we will discover that we live in a **society of Complainants**.

Look for a moment at television, and you will see that Complainants are extremely numerous: They point the finger, blaming or making the other person guilty.

EXERCISE

- Perhaps you would like to raise your hand and point your finger at another person? But notice carefully what is happening when you point one finger in the direction of the other person: There are three fingers pointing back at yourself!

- Blaming your spouse, your child, a colleague at the office, a manager or an employee serves no purpose. **The negative judgments** of another person or of yourself constitute **a form of resistance** which **leads to the persistence of problems** and difficulties.

- One of my teachers, Deepak Chopra, said: "Today I will not judge anything or anyone." And he felt new energy within himself. Yes, that liberates and makes possible tremendous progress!

- Very often we are difficult with others and with ourselves! . We are hard. Could we be **a little more cooperative**, a little more respectful of everyone in our life? Accept a little more?

CONCLUSION

To close the loop: **If the communicator sees resistance in the other person, he cannot see his efforts to cooperate. If, on the other hand, he sees his unique way of cooperating, he cannot see the resistance.**

We now come to the second-to-last chapter: **Do not change too quickly**! Here we will go more deeply into the difference between positive hypnosis and negative hypnosis.

Chapter 11

DO NOT CHANGE TOO QUICKLY!

O n visiting our planet, an extraterrestrial who was aware of the three styles of cooperation (Visitor, Complainant and Customer) would say that we are evolving in a society of Complainants. This is the form of hypnosis that we have accepted and which we are currently taking as our reality.

Accordingly, it seems important to me to come back to this subject so that we may together move away or come out of this form of self-suggestion (trance).

I have talked about hypnosis. About **positive hypnosis** ("Water the flowers...not the weeds!") and about **negative hypnosis**, by means of which we energize problems.

And we have seen, throughout the preceding chapters, that **we are all hypnotists**.

A STRATEGY FOR COMPLAINANTS

We saw that the Complainant considers himself a poor passive victim for whom nothing works on the conscious plane. A Complainant feels very helpless and generally is observed to hold many, very negative beliefs.

PASSIVE LANGUAGE

Are depressed people Customers, Complainants or Visitors? Generally Complainants! They know that there is a problem, but they are not yet ready or able to do something to solve it. A depressed person might say: "Ah! things are going badly, things are bad. I am exhausted. I am at the end of my rope. I have been depressed for three months." Very often he limits his future by adding more of the same: "I am going to be depressed for the rest of my life." **A memory in the future. A self-fulfilling prophecy**.

A depressed person maintains dysfunctional, pessimistic, negative beliefs, does he not?

When a depressed person arrives in my office or in yours, should we speak directly to his conscious mind or to his unconscious? Are we going to ask him to do something? No, because he is a poor passive victim, he can do nothing. We will use **passive language**. Depressed persons are Complainants.

PACING AND PASSIVE LANGUAGE

I will listen a lot. I will do **a lot of pacing**. The horse is in the field of problems. "I am distressed, I am depressed, things are going badly!" And often, the person might be thinking "I have been depressed for three months, I am going to be depressed for the rest of my life." Am I going to **attack this belief** directly? Am I going to **try to convince him**? Will I attempt to build up his morale?

120

What do we usually do with our spouse, an office colleague, a depressed child? Generally, we treat them as Customers. That is, we **speak directly to their conscious** mind. We try to reason with them, to make them see the good side of life and of their life in particular. But the real message that we are sending them is "It is not right, it is not OK to be depressed."

RESISTANCE LEADS TO PERSISTENCE

We struggle then against the depression and thus we reinforce it! Now when the person arrives in my office, I listen to him: "My God, it is difficult! It is not easy to have lost your job!" "It's hard to be a parent of a child with problems." I listen and I reflect back the **key words** of the person who feels at an impasse. For example, if the person tells me "It is unbearable what is happening...," I am going to reply: "I understand that you find the situation unbearable!"

The method of "parent effectiveness" teaches parents to reformulate what a child has said. With the **SFC** approach, we understand that it is important to **employ the other person's precise words**. Milton Erickson said, "Repeat the **key words** of the other person so that he will feel understood."

Key words permit us to build a relationship, to make the other feel welcomed.

After about fifteen minutes, I might say: "My dear friend, you are truly depressed. It is painful, it is exhausting. Whatever you do, don't change too quickly." And he will respond, "You can be sure of that, I won't change too quickly!"

But what have I just presupposed? That **you are already changing** and that **you will continue to change**. You are going to move out of this..." This is a **radical, significant change in that person's belief system**. A change **made indirectly on the unconscious plane**.

A VERY POWERFUL APPROACH

A person came into my office with the following beliefs: "Nothing changes in my life. I have been depressed for three months. I am going to be depressed for the rest of my life." I do **not** approach this **directly**. Instead I say, "My God, whatever you do [pacing, pacing, pacing], don't change too quickly [leading]!" Pacing and leading. **The new belief** becomes: "I am changing, but not too quickly, please." This is a very powerful intervention! Why does it work? Erickson suggests that the conscious can understand negative thoughts, but that the unconscious (which really controls, according to Erickson) does not understand negative thoughts.

We are going to do a little exercise right now. I ask you, please, **do not think of a pink elephant!** End of exercise. What did you do? You imagined and created a pink elephant because you need to create an image before you can erase it. I just gave what we call a **negative hypnotic command**. You saw that pink elephant, didn't you?

Restriction strategies are negative hypnotic commands, **hypnotic presuppositions**. Example: Do not change too quickly. One evening on television, I heard the head of a dance troupe teaching his team: "Don't do this. Don't do that, don't do this.... Especially don't do that!" He was "energizing" exactly the things that he did not want to "energize."

RESISTANCE LEADS TO PERSISTENCE!

Many parents will warn their little children "Sweetie, don't drop the glass, please!" And the child lets the glass fall! Why? Because the parent, without knowing it, has just given a **negative hypnotic command**. What is suggested to the unconscious mind is to drop the glass.

POSITIVE HYPNOSIS RATHER
THAN NEGATIVE HYPNOSIS

What the parent needs to use in this situation, is the positive formulation: "Dear, hold your glass carefully, please." You might say that this is the same thing, but the real message which is communicated is significantly different. **Water the flowers**, not the weeds. **Talk about what you want**, not about what you do not want. **"Energize" the solutions** (third generation) rather than correcting or attacking the problems (first generation). Positive hypnosis rather than negative hypnosis.

THE SWIMMING STORY

Here is a story that illustrates this very well. My sister was swimming in a pool with her son, Shaun, aged four years. She wanted to teach him to swim. But he was afraid to put his head in the water. "Come on, Shaun, you can do it!" "No! I am afraid Mama! I'm afraid, I'm scared."

She wanted to encourage him, but what did she say? "Come on, Shaun. Don't be afraid. Don't be scared." Negative hypnotic command! "No, Mom. I'm scared. I'm scared."

Helen continued, however, to encourage him. This dialogue, this argument lasted for five or ten minutes. But, fortunately, my sister, Helen, is **a solution focused mother**. Eventually she woke up and said to herself: "Oh! this isn't working!" **Elementary rule Number 3. If something is not working, A) Don't do it again! B) Do something different!** (see chapter 5)

Was this a failure for her? No, it was a learning. She realized that what she was doing with her child was not working. Therefore she changed her way of thinking and her way of intervening.

IT IS VERY SIMPLE...BUT NOT OBVIOUS!

It is very simple, but it is not obvious when we are in a vicious circle. Do you think that Shaun is a Customer for the idea of putting his head in the water? Of course not! He is a Complainant! Realizing that, Helen changed her strategy, finally saying: "Shaun, whatever you do, **don't put your head in the water too quickly!"** Suddenly little Shaun began to swim, head in the water!

Our **children**, our **spouses**, our office **colleagues**, **are always guiding** us, indicating for us **the best way of behaving and communicating with them**. We need only open our eyes and ears since, now, we possess the key (Visitor, Complainant, Customer) which enables us to not treat everyone as a Customer. This respectful typology permits us to **recognize Visitors**, **Complainants** and **Customers**. We are learning to respect these persons in their present truth, their current reality.

With a Customer, we can allow ourselves to go at high speed, to speak directly to the conscious mind. But **with Complainants**, we need to **slow down**, to **do more pacing**, and generally to speak indirectly to the unconscious mind.

WE ARE ALL HYPNOTISTS!

Do you understand that you are already marvelous hypnotists with your colleagues, your employees, your spouse and your children?

THE STORY OF THE SKI PASS

My sister and her husband are at a winter sports center. Little Shaun is wearing a cord with a season's ski pass around his neck. Shaun says to his father, "Dad, Dad, I have to pee." And David, his father, says: "You are a big boy, you are four years old now, you can go yourself. The toilet is right there but, son, when you go to the toilet, whatever you do, **don't take off your ski pass.**" Helen burst out laughing because she realized that her husband, without

124

knowing it, had just given their son a negative hypnotic command. Three minutes later, Shaun came out of the toilet without his pass. How many little children need to take off a cord hanging around their neck in order to pee?

Here again, you see the effect of negative hypnotic commands. We must pay attention to words, to our choice of words. Once again: **water the flowers, not the weeds**. The third generation uses positive hypnosis, unlike the first generation which uses negative hypnosis.

To conclude, may I ask you, dear readers,

please:

**Do not integrate
Solution Focused Communication too quickly!**

And, most importantly:

Do not have too much fun while integrating it!

Chapter 12

A Philosophy of Cooperation...
A DOLPHIN PHILOSOPHY

U p to this point, I have told many stories and I have presented many distinctions which can contribute to the enrichment of your life. Our two principal stories are "I do not have the truth" and "the Horse story." I would now like to give you one last metaphor, our third main story, "the Dolphin story." This will permit us to discover the last series of important distinctions: the three types of animals in the sea.

DOLPHINS ARE CONSIDERED TO BE THE MOST NATURALLY COOPERATIVE OF ANIMALS!

Dolphins are naturally joyful and playful. They **are naturally cooperative.** They play win-win. They are like this because they live in a world of abundance where there is enough for everyone...all the time!

This dolphin story is a good metaphor for the solution focused approach which is based on cooperation. A win-win approach, an approach of abundance.

A STORY ABOUT DOLPHINS

In San Diego, some years ago, researchers placed ninety-five sharks and five dolphins in a large pool and then left them to live together for one week. What did the researchers find in the pool a week later? Ninety-five dead sharks and five dolphins who were peacefully playing together. What had taken place? What had happened to the sharks?

The sharks had attacked each other. After some time, there were only a few sharks and five dolphins left. The sharks began to attack the dolphins. However, the dolphins wished to play with the sharks. The dolphins, we know, are naturally joyful and cooperative.

THE SHARK SEES "THE OTHER"
AS A POTENTIAL ENEMY

The psychology of the shark is the opposite of the dolphin's. The shark always sees "the other" as a potential enemy. As a potential meal!

The dolphins wished to play with the sharks in the big pool, but the sharks saw in the dolphins only potential enemies. The dolphins had tried different methods of reconciliation in order to show the sharks that they only wished to play, but the sharks attacked them unceasingly. Then, peacefully, the dolphins began to circle the sharks and when the sharks attacked, the dolphins struck their spines or they smashed their ribs. Thus it was that the sharks had drowned one after the other because of their unwillingness to play, their unwillingness to cooperate.

The authors of the book *The Strategy of the Dolphin* state that there are three types of animals in the sea: the carp, the shark and the dolphin.

THE CARP: A VICTIM FISH!

The carp is a victim fish. It is constantly being crushed by other fish. It is being eaten by the other fish.

We have all played the part of the carp in our lives. We have been more or less the victim of this or that thing, of this or that situation, of this or that person, according to the context.

THE SHARK, A WIN-LOSE STYLE!

The second category of fish is represented by the shark. The shark adopts the win-lose style: "In order that I may win, you must lose." And this, without any shading, without any distinction.

For the shark, any fish is an enemy. Any fish is a potential lunch! Perhaps we have all played this part as well or, at least, we have met sharks in our professional or personal life.

For a long time, people have said that the world of organizations where I was working was a world of sharks. From time to time, I was told stories of colleagues who would stab each other in their climb up the ladder. Or, again, I was told how they attacked other businesses, sometimes underhandedly. In short, I was observing and counseling people who were more or less in permanent competition. I was living in an inherently win-lose culture.

THE DOLPHIN, THE GREAT COLLABORATOR!

Finally, in the sea, we find a third type of animal: the **dolphin**. This great sea mammal is naturally joyous, naturally cooperative. He engages naturally in a **"win-win"** communication.

The dolphin **lives in a world of abundance**: Nothing is missing and he wishes to share with everyone.

If a dolphin is wounded, four dolphins are delegated to accompany him until he rejoins the group. Many stories are told of how dolphins have even saved human lives.

The research findings in San Diego have demonstrated that the intelligence of dolphins is greater than that of human beings. This is one of the most intelligent animals on the planet.

As we said earlier (chapter 5), we human beings are all geniuses at complicating our lives. We live in a world of sharks (win-lose). According to the United Nations, there is enough food to satisfy the needs of everyone living on the earth. However, three quarters of the population are starving to death and there are more wars now on the planet than there have ever been in the entire history of humankind. Human beings are killing each other.

THE SHARK LIVES IN A WORLD OF POVERTY!

Solution Focused Communication gives us **enriching distinctions** which help us to enlighten both our professional and, in a different way, our personal life. **The shark makes no distinctions.** Consequently he lives in a world that is poor and restricted. A world where, in order that he may win, others must die or lose.

Sharks make no distinction between sharks and dolphins. All other beings are potential enemies. You know that sharks fight among themselves, that they can devour each other.

A law of cybernetics reveals that it is the most flexible person who will have the advantage in any situation, whatever it may be.

THE DOLPHIN IS A GREAT DEAL MORE FLEXIBLE BECAUSE HE LIVES IN A WORLD FULL OF ENRICHING DISTINCTIONS!

What happens when a shark meets a dolphin? The shark attacks: "I live in a world of poverty; win-lose, I am going to devour you, I am going to kill you." The dolphin is more flexible. He defends himself with subtlety, he escapes, then he invites the other animal to play his game of life: **"I live in a world of** wealth and **abundance** from all points of view. I play the game of life. **I am cooperative.** I am joyful. In the sea, there is plenty for everyone. **I play win-win**. Do you want to play with me? And the shark attacks again. His fish psychology shouts: **"Win-lose**, poverty, I am going to eat you immediately. I am afraid of losing something!"

I AM FLEXIBLE ENOUGH TO BECOME A SHARK WHEN IT IS APPROPRIATE!

Once more the dolphin escapes. His language is "Abundance, **win-win,** play, cooperation." And the shark – who has not learned Solution Focused Communication which the dolphin knows naturally – attacks.

The shark says: "We live in a sea of **winners and losers.** A sea of poverty." The dolphin escapes, repeating: "Let's celebrate the abundance of our sea. Let's play **win-win. Let's cooperate!"** The shark does not have at his disposal the inner resources to go beyond his narrow vision; he therefore attacks again. The dolphin, seeing that there is nothing else to do, then affirms, **"I am flexible enough to become a shark when it is appropriate."** And he adjusts in order to confront and kill the shark.

Do you see? This is very important. **Enlightened people,** naturally "dolphin (win-win)," **know** how to play **"win-lose"** when it is necessary!

A "BEGINNER" (NEWBORN) DOLPHIN

If by chance, and this is very rare, the shark has the intelligence to understand that he cannot beat the dolphin and is open to the dolphin game of cooperation, the dolphin **will easily forgive him** and play with the "beginner" dolphin. When the shark begins to cooperate, to play the game of life (win-win), the dolphin treats him spontaneously as if he were a dolphin.

PSEUDO-ENLIGHTENED CARPS

We can all recognize these different types of fish among ourselves. In the book referred to, it is also stated that there are many pseudo-enlightened carps among us. That is to say, we perceive ourselves as dolphins, but, from time to time, we are a little **too nice for our own good** and thus are crushed by the sharks.

To "dolphinize" organizations, couples and families!

My objective, throughout this book and through the seminars that I give, is to **"dolphinize"** businesses, organizations, institutions, schools, families and couples.

At various levels, we are all **dolphins in training**!

The story of the dolphins reveals to us, above all, that we are not limited to one particular style of behavior. According to the requirements of the moment, we have the necessary **flexibility** to play the three roles. We can become sharks in order to stop things that are unacceptable. Dolphins know how to do this. This does not prevent us from again becoming dolphins later on.

Ideally, like the "beginner" dolphin, we adopt as much as possible the natural dolphin style: **cooperative, playful, win-win, abundance.**

132

CONCLUSION

Dear readers, we have just presented an overview, an introduction, a sensitization to the Solution Focused Communication approach. Amongst colleagues, we say that this approach is:

Number 1: **A way of thinking**. Ex.: I do not have the truth (chapter 1); Third generation (chapter 2); The metabeliefs (chapters 3 and 4); Ericksonian principles (chapter 8).

Number 2: **A way of having a conversation**. Ex.: The miracle-question (chapter 3), the exception-question, the scaling-questions (chapter 5).

Number 3: **A way of intervening**. Ex.: The three elementary rules, the tasks (chapter 5), Pacing and Leading (chapters 9 and 10).

But above all, **the SFC approach** is a **philosophy, a way of being, an attitude**. I have often said to my participants that it is this way of being, or this attitude (this system of beliefs), which is our principal gift to others and to ourselves!

During a day of supervision, one participant said to me, "I have not mastered the SFC techniques, I have only integrated **the philosophy**." I burst out laughing and I answered: "If you have the philosophy, that is **the most important thing**! The techniques will come by themselves!"

In another seminar, a colleague asked me, "Does this approach apply everywhere in all situations?" Being a good cheerleader of the third generation, I returned the question: "What do you think?" He replied, "Not necessarily all the techniques, but **the spirit of the SFC approach can be applied all the time**, in any professional or personal situation!"

What we have presented in this book, is first of all **a philosophy of cooperation** – an approach of **acceptance** or **non-resistance**. We have talked a great deal about the importance of **our beliefs** and of **our presuppositions** to help us dance with life instead of pushing in another direction. Most importantly, we have recognized that **resistance leads to persistence**.

As a result, most of the **ideas and techniques** presented here are **"energized" by this spirit of acceptance** and of non-resistance.

OUR FUNDAMENTAL BELIEFS:

1. The Serenity Prayer

2. The situation in which you find yourself at this moment is perfect for your growth!

SOME IMPORTANT QUESTIONS to ask yourself:

1. Do you have problems or **opportunities**?

2. Do you experience failures or **learnings**?

3. Do you live in a world where there is only **one truth or many**?

4. Is there only **one solution** or are there **thousands**?

5. Do you live in a world where others resist you, where

they are not motivated and non-cooperative, or do you live in a world where each person has **his unique way of cooperating** (Visitor, Complainant, Customer) you can recognize and use so as to better cooperate with him or her?

6. Do you use negative hypnosis or **positive hypnosis**?

7. Finally, do you **WATER THE FLOWERS** or the weeds?

At this time, I would like to thank you, dear readers, for your curiosity and for your openness of spirit, and I would like to conclude with one last story.

THE STORY OF THE COVERED WAGONS

This story took place in America during the 1850s. At that time, a law voted by the United States Congress authorized new arrivals, immigrants, to travel toward the center of the continent, where they would receive free grants of land if they were prepared to do the necessary work to make them livable.

On learning that, one family who was living on the East coast at Philadelphia took all their belongings in a covered wagon and undertook a long trip of five or six months, arriving finally in the middle of the continent, in Kansas.

The travelers stopped near a stream in order to feed the animals and the children. By chance, they met an old farmer who had been living in the area for forty years. The head of the family then asked the old farmer the following questions:

"What is it like in this region? You have been here a long time? Is it a good place to plant our seeds, to build our farm and to raise our children? How are the people here? Are they kind? Are they good? Are they cooperative?"

The old farmer was a solution focused man. Accordingly, he replied with a question: "What were the people like in the East where you came from?"

The head of the family replied: "Oh! They were disgusting, depressing, dreadful, not at all cooperative!"

After listening, the old farmer replied: "I am sorry to inform you that **it is exactly like that here**. It would be better to continue your voyage and to look elsewhere for your new home."

Two weeks later, a second family arrived in the same region. These travelers had also come from the East with their covered wagon. They also had traveled for a long time. Finally they arrived in Kansas. By chance, they stopped at the same stream where the first family had camped. They fed the animals and the children and, again by chance, they met the same old farmer.

Like the first family, they asked the questions: "What is it like in this area? Is it a good place to plant our seeds, to build our farm, to bring up our children and to begin a new life? How are the people here? Are they kind, good, cooperative?"

The old farmer, still solution focused, replied with the same question: "What were the people like in the East?" This second family replied: Oh! they were very kind, very nice, very helpful, very cooperative!"

The old farmer looked at them and then replied: "**It is exactly like that here**. My dear neighbors, welcome to your new land!"

Dear readers, dear gardeners, dear dolphins-in-training, welcome to your new planet where you can now choose a little more often to **WATER THE FLOWERS**, not the weeds.

SUMMARY

A PHILOSOPHY OF COOPERATION ORIENTED TOWARD A POSITIVE PERCEPTION OF LIFE

COMMON LANGUAGE

Water the flowers...

The principal person that you can help...yourself

Bring back the horse...

Visitor, Complainant, Customer

Pacing and leading

(Slow down to speed up)

Do your best with positive intention

Resistance >>> Persistence

"The OK-ness principle"

The Serenity Prayer

CHANGE YOUR TAPE

"I do not have the truth"

The three generations of communication

Carry the horse less

No failures...only learnings

Problems >>> Opportunities

A unique way of cooperating

Not just one solution but thousands

And what else?

Don't change too quickly...

The style of the dolphin

QUESTIONS

1. Miracle
2. Exception
3. Scaling

TASKS

Observe.... Continue.... When?
Do more of what works...
Do something different...

THOUGHTS TO REMEMBER...

1. The situation in which you find yourself at this moment
   is perfect for your growth, for your learning and for
   your flowering.

2. The quality of your life is proportional to the quality of
   your questions...and of the distinctions that you make...

3. More and more, I do less and less...

INTEGRATION EXERCISE

How can you integrate
SOLUTION FOCUSED COMMUNICATION
into your life?

1. **What aspects** of this book are the **most useful** and pertinent for you?

2. **How, specifically, are you going to apply them?**

3. **What advantages** in the short term/in the medium term/in the long term **will you draw from it?**

4. **How can you** (are you going to) **ensure the followup** of this book?

BIBLIOGRAPHY

Chopra, D. **Unconditional Life**. New York: Bantan, 1991.

De Shazer, S. **Clues, Investigating Solutions**. New York: Norton, 1988.

De Shazer, S. **Keys to Solutions**. New York: Norton, 1985.

Fisch, R., J. Weakland, and L. Segal. **The Tactics of Change**. San Francisco: Josey Bass, 1982.

Haley, J. **Uncommon Therapy: Milton H. Erickson**. New York: Norton,1973.

Keyes, K. **Handbook to Higher Consciousness**. Coos Bay, Or.: The Vision Foundation, 1972.

Kral, R. **Strategies that Work, Techniques for Solutions in the Schools**. Milwaukee, Wis.: Brief Family Therapy Center, 1988.

Lynch, D. et P. Kordis. **The Strategy of the Dolphin**. New York: Fawcett, 1988.

Oakley, E. and D. Krug. **Enlightened Leadership**. New York: Simon & Shuster 1993.

O'Hanlon, W. H. and M. Weiner-Davis. **In Search of Solutions, A New Direction**. New York: Norton, 1989.

Peacock, F. **Basic Ericksonian Principles**. Master's Thesis, Montreal, McGill University, 1987.

Robbins, A. **Awaken the Giant Within**. New York: Summit, 1991.

Roman, S. **Living With Joy**. Tiburon, Calif.: Kramer, 1986.

Walter, J. L. and J. Peller. **Becoming Solution-Focused**. New York: Brunner/Mazel, 1992.

YOU HAVE ENJOYED THIS BOOK AND WOULD LIKE TO
INVITE THE AUTHOR INTO YOUR COMMUNITY
OR INTO YOUR ORGANIZATION?

For more information on the seminars, keynote addresses and training sessions given by the author, you can communicate directly with:

Fletcher Peacock Enterprises Inc.
1235 Bernard St. West, Suite 17
Montreal, Quebec
Canada
H2V 1V7
Telephone: (514) 495-3699
Fax: (514) 495-3699
E-mail: solution1@videotron.ca
Web site: www.FletcherPeacockCommunicationSolutions.com

Complete the form on the following page and mail it to the above address. You will receive a folder containing detailed information on Fletcher Peacock's courses.

Fletcher Peacock gives **seminars**, **workshops** and **keynote addresses** in **Canada** and in many major cities in **North America**. Also presented **to Europeans**, these training sessions can be given in **French or in English** and are available especially to groups (organizations, business, institutions) and also to individuals who wish to improve their skills to better communicate with everyone in their environment.

All the teachings presented in this book are taken and enriched with examples, exercises and put into practical situations which permit them to **be integrated more fully** into everyday life. Endowed with an **extraordinary talent for popularizing**, Fletcher Peacock presents lively, creative, interactive workshops with **enthusiasm, freshness, dynamism** and **humor**.

Name: _____

Business/Organization?/Community: _____

_____

Position: _____

Address: _____

_____

_____

Telephone: _____

Fax: _____

E-mail: _____

I would like to receive more information: Yes _____No _____

I would like to explore the possibility of inviting the author to my organization and/or my community: Yes _____No _____